From ACADIA
to YELLOWSTONE

From ACADIA *to* YELLOWSTONE

THE NATIONAL PARKS OF THE UNITED STATES

PRINCIPAL PHOTOGRAPHY BY J. A. KRAULIS

ADDITIONAL PHOTOGRAPHY BY RALPH BRUNNER AND DAVID MUENCH

SMITHMARK

This edition published in 1996 by SMITHMARK publishers, a division of U.S. Media Holdings, Inc., 16 East 32nd Street, New York, NY 10016.

SMITHMARK books are available for bulk purchase for sales promotion and premium use. For details write or call the manager of special sales, SMITHMARK Publishers, 16 East 32nd Street, New York, NY 10016; (212) 532-6600.

Produced by
Key Porter Books Limited
70 The Esplanade
Toronto, Ontario
M5E 1R2

ISBN 0-8317-6229-2

Printed and bound in Hong Kong

10 9 8 7 6 5 4 3 2 1

PAGE 1: Clearing weather above Arrigetch Creek, Gates of the Arctic National Park and Preserve.

PAGE 3: Washer Woman Arch and Monster Tower seen through Mesa Arch at sunrise, Canyonlands National Park.

PAGE 5: Sun-baked mud and sand dunes near Stovepipe Wells, Death Valley National Park.

PAGE 6: Dusk silhouettes a juniper and a skyline of assorted alpine conifers near Tenaya Lake, Yosemite National Park.

PAGE 12: The soft, graceful landscape of the Mesquite Flat Dunes is a contrast to the raw, rough geology typical of the rest of Death Valley National Park.

PAGE 13: Part of the city of vivid hoodoos visible from Sunrise Point, Bryce Canyon National Park.

PAGE 14: A juniper complements the view of Soda Springs Basin, the White Rim, and Stillwater Canyon from the Green River Overlook, Canyonlands National Park.

PAGE 15: Looking down from the South Rim near Hopi Point, Grand Canyon National Park.

PAGE 16: Waterfalls along the Northern Circuit, a popular three- or four-day backpack in Mount Rainier National Park.

PAGE 17: The view from Beauty Pool takes in columns of steam venting from the numerous fumaroles, hot springs and geysers of Upper Geyser Basin, Yellowstone National Park.

PAGE 18: Sections of a 250-million-year-old stone "log" lie scattered amid recently eroded badlands near Blue Mesa, Petrified Forest National Park.

PAGE 19: Redwoods soar into the mists and out of sight at Lady Bird Johnson Grove, Redwood National Park.

PAGE 160: The Tetons reflected in Jackson Lake at sunrise, Grand Teton National Park

Contents

National Parks of the United States

North Cascades●
Olympic●
Mount Rainier● WA
Glacier●
Voyageurs●
Isle Royale●
ME
Acadia●

Crater Lake● OR
MT
ND
MN
Lake Superior
VT NH
Lassen Volcanic●
ID
●Yellowstone
●Grand Teton
WY
SD
●Badlands
●Wind Cave
WI
Lake Michigan
MI
Lake Huron
Lake Ontario
NY
Lake Erie
MA
CT
RI
PA
NJ

Redwood●
NV
●Yosemite
CA
Great Basin●
UT
Arches●
Rocky Mountain●
●Canyonlands
Capitol Reef●
●Bryce Canyon
●Kings Canyon
CO
IA
NE
IL
IN
OH
Washington DC
MD
DE
WV
Shenandoah●
VA

Sequoia●
●Death Valley
●Zion
●Mesa Verde
KS
MO
KY
Mammoth Cave●
Grand Canyon●
●Channel Islands
TN
●Great Smoky Mountains
NC
Joshua Tree●
AZ
Petrified●
Forest
OK
AR
SC
NM
Hot Springs●
Saguaro●
●Carlsbad Caverns
●Guadalupe Mountains
TX
LA
MS
AL
GA
FL

●Gates of the Arctic
●Kobuk Valley
Denali●
Wrangell-St. Elias●
Lake Clark●
●Kenai
Fjords
Glacier Bay●
Katmai●
AK

Big Bend●

Everglades● ●Biscayne
Dry Tortugas●
●American Samoa

Puerto Virgin Islands●
Rico
Virgin Islands

Haleakala●
Hawaii Volcanoes●
HI

9

Acknowledgments

The editors wish to acknowledge the invaluable assistance of the U.S. National Park Service in the preparation of this book. Further, they would like to thank Rosa Wilson of the Park Service's photographic library for her persistence in tracking down many of the harder-to-find images contained within this book. Linda Meyers, at the Division of Publications, and Christopher Soller, at the Office of Legislative Affairs, kindly offered help with primary and the latest information on the parks.

Introduction

On August 25, 1916, President Woodrow Wilson signed the act creating the National Park Service, then a new federal bureau in the Department of the Interior responsible for protecting some 40 existing national parks and monuments, along with others to be established in the future. In essence, the National Park Service has set out since then to be the guardian of thousands of vast and diverse natural resources that are accessible to – and for the enjoyment of – the public. In all, the National Park System now comprises 367 areas covering more than 80 million acres in 49 states.

The nomenclature used to describe these areas varies. Generally speaking, a national park contains a variety of resources and encompasses large land or water areas. Areas added to the National Park System because of their natural attributes or other distinctive characteristics are usually designated as monuments, preserves, seashores, lakeshores, and riverways. A national monument is intended to preserve at least one nationally significant resource and is usually smaller than a national park and lacks its range of attractions. A number of national monuments have been "upgraded" to become national parks. National preserves are designed for the protection of certain resources. National seashores and lakeshores focus on the preservation of areas near water and focus on providing water-oriented recreation. National rivers and wild scenic riverways preserve stretches of land bordering on free-flowing streams that have not been dammed, channelized, or otherwise altered. These areas provide opportunities for hiking, canoeing, and hunting.

More than half of the areas in the National Park System preserve places and commemorate persons, events, and activities important in the nation's history. These areas are referred to as national historic sites, national military parks, and national battlefield sites.

This book's focus is on the national parks themselves, and includes all 54 that are currently sprinkled across the nation. The editors of this book trust that you will take the time to explore the many facets of America's wonderful public outdoor places and will use this book both as an inspiration and a departure point for many trips to come. Along the way, readers will discover the hundreds of other areas that make up the National Park System and hopefully will come to appreciate the efforts being taken to preserve and protect America's valuable recreational resources.

Acadia National Park

A morning view of Atlantic waters from the top of Cadillac Mountain, the first place in the National Park System lit by the rising sun.

With 300 species of birds, Acadia National Park is a bird-watcher's paradise. This seaside park offers a wonderful setting in which to sit on a rocky ledge or stony beach and relax, watching herring gulls sail overhead and breathing in the fresh salt air. The park – where land and sea meet – abounds in wildlife, from the rugged coastal area of Mount Desert Island to the picturesque Schoodic Peninsula on the mainland and the spectacular cliffs of Isle au Haut.

Little of New England's rock-bound coast remains in public ownership, undeveloped and natural. Acadia preserves the natural beauty of part of Maine's coast, its coastal mountains, and its offshore islands. Weather permitting, you can drive to the top of Cadillac Mountain, the highest point here, for a spectacular view of this coast. The sights can also be enjoyed by walking or biking on more than 120 miles of trails winding through the park.

Acadia, as the name suggests, was French before it was English and then American. The French and English battled for possession of North America from 1613 until 1760. French frigates hid from English men-of-war in Frenchman Bay, screened by the Porcupine Islands. When French explorer Samuel de Champlain sailed into the bay in 1604, he named Mount Desert Island for its landmark bare top.

The sea encircles, thrusts inland, and fogs here. In the midday sun, its bright-blue surface is studded with lobster buoys. In fog, all is gray and muted. Somewhere out at sea a lobster boat's engines may mutter, but the boat is barely visible, lost in a formless world. Seen at sundown from Cadillac Mountain, the sea glows soft pink, mauve, and gold. Gulls wing silently home to distant islands, and, like fireflies, navigational aids flash warnings

ACADIA NATIONAL PARK
Established 1919
41,933 acres
P.O. Box 177
Bar Harbor, ME 04609
(207) 288-3338

from reefs, islands, and headland. Between the sea and the forested mountains here is the small, fascinating, almost netherworld of the tidal zone. Twice daily exposed to air and drowned by seawater, it is a world of specially adapted organisms. Tidepools, pockets of seawater stranded in rock basins at low tide, are microhabitats brimming with life. In these natural aquariums, green sea urchins and other marine creatures go about their business. This zone of life is illustrated here by Acadia's tides, which vary from 9 to 14 feet, averaging 11 to 12 feet. It is the primeval meeting place of earth and water.

Behind the sea lie Acadia's forests and mountains, made accessible for exploring by an extensive system of carriage roads. These broad, smooth, graveled byways encircle Jordan Pond and Eagle Lake and wind around the flanks of Sargent and Penobscot mountains. They offer stunning views of Somes Sound and Frenchman Bay, and they lead you along beaver-dammed brooks. The grades are gentle, but the vistas are long. The loop around Eagle Lake is a bicycle path.

The story of the people who lived on this island when Champlain first saw it is told in the Abbé Museum at Sieur de Monts Spring with Indian artifacts and exhibits. Islesford Museum, on Little Cranberry Island, houses ship models, tools, and pictures that reveal island life in the nineteenth and early twentieth centuries.

Villages near the park present the variety of lifestyles on the island today. Northeast Harbor shelters sailboats, large and small, and a summer colony. Bar Harbor caters to tourists, offering many accommodations and amusements. Bass Harbor and Southwest Harbor, and Winter Harbor at Schoodic, retain more of the traditional flavor of Maine coastal villages. Those who earn their living from the sea – whether at lobstering, fishing, building boats, or guarding the coast – tie up here. And canneries, lobster pounds, and boatyards have not yet been replaced by summer homes and motels.

Acadia offers wonderful opportunities for exploring marine environments. On the tidepool walks offered by National Park Service naturalists, you can learn about plants and animals in the microhabitats between land and sea. On cruises led by a naturalist, you may get to see porpoises, seals, eagles, and nesting colonies of seabirds. Or you may get to watch an osprey catch a fish and cart it off to its nest of hungry young-

sters. On an offshore island, you can reflect on the lonely life of a lighthouse keeper's family. These are only a few of the scenic, natural, historical, and recreational attractions of Acadia.

Acadia National Park is unusual because it was neither carved out of public lands nor bought with public funds. It was envisioned by and donated through the efforts of many private citizens who loved Mount Desert Island, Schoodic Peninsula, and the nearby islands. Maine residents and summer visitors alike donated their time and resources to preserve Acadia's beauty. George B. Dorr and Charles W. Eliot, a former president of Harvard University, saw the dangers of development and acted to avoid them. John D. Rockefeller, Jr., also played a critical role. He built the carriage roads and gave more than 11,000 acres, about one-third of the park's area, to what became known as Acadia National Park.

National Park of American Samoa

This park's rain forest is surrounded by a sparkling azure sea. Vic Vaiva Bay is pictured here.
(NATIONAL PARK SERVICE)

One of America's newest national parks preserves not only the tropical rain forest of American-Samoan volcanic islands, but also the unique relationship of the Polynesians to their land, which they named "Samoa," meaning "sacred earth." The 4,000-year-old culture of the Samoans, the oldest of the Polynesians, remains closely tied to this South Pacific island environment.

This remote park lies some 2,300 miles southwest of Honolulu, in the unincorporated U.S. territory of American Samoa. The park protects Tutuila, Ta'u, and Ofu, three of the seven islands of American Samoa, and the surrounding waters extending to a pristine coral reef.

Authorized in 1988, when Samoan tribal chiefs agreed to lease parts of their land, the National Park of American Samoa was established in 1993, when the National Park Service and the governor of American Samoa signed a fifty-year lease agreement. This arrangement ensures that the park will not change the communal ownership of land passed down the generations by oral tradition and custom. Villages and communities continue to own and control land within the park's boundaries, and Samoans can still practice traditional plant-gathering and subsistence activities.

Though not the only American tropical rain forest, American Samoa's, which includes forests of lowland, montane, coast, ridge, and cloud, features a unique paleotropical ecosystem. The park's rain forest and the surrounding azure sea are home to a diversity of tropical animals, including the flying fox, a fruit bat with a three-foot wingspan; the Pacific boa; green and hawksbill sea tortoises; geckos and skinks; and an array of birds and fish.

The forces of natural disasters and man have substantially altered an estimated two-thirds of the native vegetation of the Samoan archipelago. The park, the island of Ta'u in particular, preserves the greatest diversity of native vegetation in Samoa. Most of the estimated 380 species of native plants and 120 naturalized species, and nearly half of the native flowers, flourish within the park's boundaries. However, if the native forests of western Samoa continue to be exploited at today's pace, they will probably be destroyed within ten years. Much of the wildlife found in American Samoa today was introduced by man, such as the marine toad and the house gecko. The only land mammals native to Samoa are three species of bats. Two species of flying foxes pollinate plants and disperse seeds in the park's rain forest, and are crucial for the forest's survival. But hunting and hurricanes have dramatically decreased the numbers of the endangered flying foxes. Several species of birds are also endangered, including four species of pigeons and fruit doves hunted by Samoans for subsistence. The Pacific boa, the only snake in American Samoa, lives only on the island of Ta'u, within the park. The rare green and hawksbill sea turtles nest on the white sandy beaches of the park. The coral reef on Ofu island, one of the few preserved reefs of the Samoa islands, is alive with 150 species of coral, three times the number of species found in reefs in the Caribbean national parks.

The National Park of American Samoa preserves the pristine beauty of these South Pacific islands, featuring a lush rain forest and steep volcanic mountains plunging down to meet the deep-blue ocean waves that wash up against miles of quiet coves and beaches. But apart from this breathtaking landscape, the park includes two of the oldest known archaeological sites in American Samoa and seeks to preserve the traditions and customs of the Samoan culture.

NATIONAL PARK OF AMERICAN SAMOA
Established 1993
9,000 acres
National Park of American Samoa
Pago Pago, American Samoa 96799
(808) 541-2693

Arches National Park

Arches National Park boasts not only the greatest density of natural arches in the world, but also a spectacular display of massive balanced rocks, spires, pinnacles, and pedestals set against a vast sky. More than 1,500 arches have been catalogued, ranging in size from a 3-foot opening (the minimum considered an arch) to Landscape Arch, which measures 306 feet from base to base.

The peculiar rock formations were sculpted by the elements – wind, water, extreme temperatures, and underground salt movement. When the sky is clear blue, it is hard to imagine such violent forces – 100 million years of erosion of sandstone – creating this seemingly timeless landscape. But all stages of decay and arch formation are found here. In 1991 a slab of rock about 60 feet long, 11 feet wide, and 4 ½ feet thick fell from the underside of Landscape Arch,

Behind Navajo Arch, a narrow, secluded alcove gives a cliff-framed view of the sky.

leaving behind an even thinner ribbon of rock. Delicate Arch, an isolated remnant of a bygone fin formation (a vertical rock slab), stands on the brink of a canyon, with the dramatic La Sal Mountains for a backdrop.

Among the impressive sights are South Park Avenue Trailhead, an array of balanced rocks perched atop seemingly inadequate bases, spires, and eroded fins that resemble a city skyline; the world-famous Balanced Rock; The Windows section, consisting of four large arches; and Panorama Point, providing a vista of Salt Valley and of the Fiery Furnace, a series of parallel red fins.

The park, bordered in part by the Colorado River, lies in Utah's southeastern red rock country. Five miles from the Mormon pioneer town of Moab, Utah, the park is also near Canyonlands National Park; Dead Horse Point State Park; Colorado, Dinosaur, and Natural Bridges national monuments; and Glen Canyon National

ARCHES NATIONAL PARK
Established 1971
73,379 acres
P.O. Box 907
Moab, UT 84532
(801) 259-8161

Recreation Area.

Wolfe Ranch – a typical early-West cattle operation – provides a glimpse into the past. John Wesley Wolfe, a disabled Civil War veteran, and his son, Fred, settled here in 1888. A weathered log cabin, a root cellar, and the corral remain as evidence of their primitive ranch.

Arches National Park lies atop an underground salt bed, which was the primary force in the creation of the arches and spires, balanced rocks, sandstone fins, and eroded monoliths that attract sightseers. Thousands of feet thick in places, this salt bed was deposited over the Colorado Plateau some 300 million years ago, when a sea flowed into the region and eventually evaporated. Over millions of years, the salt bed was covered with residue from floods and

winds and oceans. Much of the debris was compressed into rock. At one time, this overlying earth may have been 1 mile thick.

Salt under pressure is unstable, and the salt bed below Arches was no match for the weight of this thick cover of rock. Under such pressure it shifted, buckled, liquefied, and repositioned itself, thrusting the Earth's layers upward into domes. Whole sections dropped into cavities, and in places turned almost on edge. Faults occurred. The result of one such 2,500-foot displacement, the Moab Fault, can be seen from the visitor center.

As this subsurface movement of salt shaped the Earth, surface erosion stripped away the younger rock layers. Except for isolated remnants, the major formations visible in the park today are the salmon-colored Entrada sandstone, in which most of the arches form, and the buff-colored Navajo sandstone. These are visible in layer-cake formation throughout most of the park. Over time, water seeped into the superficial cracks, joints, and folds of these layers. Ice formed in the fissures,

expanding and putting pressure on surrounding rock, breaking off bits and pieces. Winds later cleaned out the loose particles. A series of freestanding fins remained. Wind and water attacked these fins until, in some, the cementing material gave way and chunks of rock tumbled out. Many damaged fins collapsed. Others, with the right degree of hardness and balance, survived despite their missing sections. These became the famous arches.

This is the geologic story of Arches – probably. The evidence is largely circumstantial.

Much of the park consists of rugged stone, but the landscape is not barren. Pinyon pines and gnarled juniper trees add a splash of green contrast to the red sandstone terrain. Desert flora abound in the park. In spring, when conditions are right, wildflowers bloom in profusion. From April to July, colorful displays carpet moist places.

Wildlife is characteristic of the

Along with arches, sandstone rock towers are numerous in The Windows section of the park.

sparse pinyon-and-juniper forest communities of the Great Basin Desert. Most species are nocturnal, but visitors might see a mule deer, kit fox, or, more often, jackrabbits and cottontails, kangaroo rats and other rodents, and small reptiles. Flocks of blue pinyon jays live here, and mountain bluebirds and many other migratory species pass through the park. Arches is also home to golden eagles and red-tailed hawks, and bald eagles and peregrine falcons have also been sighted here.

RIGHT: Desert paintbrush grows along Winter Camp Wash near Delicate Arch.

FAR RIGHT: The main opening of Turret Arch frames another arch, South Window, in the distance.

Badlands National Park

This magnificent scene shows the Badlands' characteristic dry, stark landscape. (RALPH BRUNNER)

The Sioux called this seemingly inhospitable southwestern South Dakota landscape *mako sica*, or "bad land." So, too, the French fur trappers called the region the *mauvaises terres à traverser*, meaning "bad lands to travel across." More recently, Badlands National Park has come to be appreciated for its striking beauty. In *Dances with Wolves*, Kevin Costner's epic film about a Civil War soldier who befriends a Sioux Indian tribe, this arid terrain, with its steep canyons, sharp ridges, gullies, spires, and knobs, became a breathtaking backdrop.

Out of the Dakota prairie, rain, wind, and frost have carved this rough terrain. Not only has erosion created a new landscape, it has also bared rocks laid down as sediments during the Eocene and Oligocene epochs, between 37 and 23 million years ago, revealing a record of the past.

At the close of the Eocene (40 to 45 million years ago), this land was a broad marshy plain crossed by sluggish streams flowing from highlands to the west. As the Oligocene epoch drew to a close, volcanoes to the west and southwest ejected huge volumes of ash into the atmosphere. Borne eastward by the winds, the ash fell and became the whitish layer near the top of the Badlands formations. Slowly the climate began to change, and increasingly dry winds blew from the north. Rainfall diminished. Grass, able to grow with less water, invaded and occupied the drying realms of forest and swamps. The animals changed, too, with grass-eaters and those able to withstand a more vigorous climate coming to the fore and other species disappearing. The water that today eats into the soft Badlands formations falls mostly as rain during torrential spring and summer storms. Nonetheless, current annual precipitation, including the storms, is only 16 inches, just enough to sustain the grass.

Despite summer temperatures that may top 100°F, and frigid winter winds, many animals and plants still find the Badlands a good place to live. White-throated swifts and cliff swallows nest on the faces of cliffs, and rock wrens build in the crevices. An occasional pair of golden eagles may rear their young on a high, inaccessible butte. Along the drainages and passes, junipers patch the landscape with green. Yuccas dot the broken slopes and valleys. Islands of life collect where water is found. There cottonwoods, wild roses, skunkbush sumac, and other trees and shrubs shelter birds. Wherever trees and shrubs grow, porcupines, chipmunks,

mice, and even bats are sure to live. Here and there hundreds of prairie dogs busily attend to the affairs of their towns. Badgers and coyotes lurk nearby, ready to make a meal of one of them. Jackrabbits and cottontails bound through the swaying grass. And prairie rattlesnakes, yellow-bellied racers, and bullsnakes ripple along in search of prey.

BADLANDS NATIONAL PARK
Established 1978
242,756 acres
P.O. Box 6
Interior, SD 57750
(605) 433-5361

The great nineteenth-century influx of immigrants from eastern America doomed some of the large mammals of the plains – the gray wolf, the elk, the grizzly bear. Others, the mule deer and the pronghorn, decreased in numbers before rebounding. Bison and Audubon's bighorn sheep were exterminated from the Badlands. The National Park Service, seeking to restore the vanished prairie,

reintroduced bison and a close relative of the bighorn, and they are doing well.

Though seemingly forbidding at first glance, the Badlands has supported humans for more than 12,000 years. The area's earliest people were ancient mammoth-hunters. Much later they were followed by tribes whose lives centered on bison-hunting. The Arikara were the first Indian tribe known to have inhabited the White River area. By the mid-eighteenth century, they were replaced by the Sioux, or Lakota, who dominated the region. Though the bison-hunting Lakota flourished during the next 100 years, their dominion on the prairie was short-lived. French fur trappers were the first of many European arrivals who, in time, would supplant the Lakota. Trappers were soon followed by soldiers, miners, cattlemen, and homesteaders who forever changed the face of the prairie. After 40 years of struggle, culminating in the 1890 Wounded Knee Massacre, the Lakota were confined to reservations. Cattle replaced bison; wheat replaced prairie; and, in time, gasoline-powered vehicles

replaced the horse.

Before long, the Badlands came to be regarded more as a geologic wonder worthy of preservation than as a wasteland. Authorized by Congress in 1929, Badlands National Monument was proclaimed by President Franklin D. Roosevelt in 1939 to preserve the scenery, to protect the fossils and wildlife, and to conserve the mixed-grass prairie. The size of the monument more than doubled in 1976, with the addition of 133,300 acres of the Pine Ridge Reservation, to be administered by the National Park Service in agreement with the Oglala Sioux Tribe. Called the "Stronghold Unit" (including the detached Palmer Creek Unit), this stunning landscape of high grassy tableland and spectacular buttes is the scene of much Lakota history. The Ghost Dances at Stronghold Table in 1890 were a prelude to the bloodshed at Wounded Knee, 25 miles south of the White River Visitor Center. Congress elevated the status of Badlands National Monument to Badlands National Park in 1978, underscoring the value of the Badlands to present and future generations.

Big Bend National Park

The Indians said that after making the Earth, the Great Spirit simply dumped all the leftover rocks on the Big Bend. Spanish explorers, less intimate with the landscape, merely dubbed this "the uninhabited land." To come to know this land of desert and mountains, cut through by the Rio Grande, the "big river," is but to grasp at a larger appreciation of the unknown. Here you will find, believe it or not, a desert amphibian, Couch's spadefoot toad; a mosquito fish whose entire world range is one pond in the park; a small mammal, the kangaroo rat, which metabolizes water from carbohydrates in seeds; and a good-sized bird, the roadrunner, that would rather run than fly. There are winged insects that live their entire lives in, on, and off one species of plant. By contrast, coyotes may turn up anywhere and will eat almost anything. Jackrabbits have such large ears that they use them as radiators, transferring body heat to the environment.

These diverse species live within the three natural divisions of Big Bend: the river, the desert, and the mountains. The name "Big Bend" refers to the great U-turn the Rio Grande makes here in southwest Texas, separating the United States from Mexico and defining the park's southern boundary for 118 miles. The river is an arcing linear oasis, a ribbon of green strung across the dry desert and cutting through its mountains. Much of the water flowing through the park is supplied by the Rio Conchos, flowing out of Mexico; a significant amount of the water of the Rio Grande is diverted for irrigation or lost to evaporation before reaching the park's western boundary. The garfish and some turtles in the river are living fossils that help describe the area's former life as a lush savannah and swamp 50 million years ago, when their

Parry's agave, the century plant – so named because many years pass before it blossoms, but once, and then dies – and the Chisos Mountains.

ancestors swam in company with crocodiles and hippopotamus-like creatures.

Among the most startling sights in this desert country may be the tooth marks of beaver on cottonwood or willow trees along the river. But don't look for beaver lodges. The beaver in the Big Bend live in bank burrows. The river is an oasis for species not adapted to the aridity of desert life, and thus adds to the park's biological diversity.

The river floodplain provides good areas for bird-watchers. Some birders maintain that the birds in the floodplain are more colorful than elsewhere. Here you may find summer tanagers, painted buntings, vermilion flycatchers, and cardinals serving as accent colors to the background greens of floodplain foliage. This ribbon-like floodplain verdancy, seen from a distance, appears as a green belt in the desert. It is a phe-

BIG BEND NATIONAL PARK
Established 1944
801,163 acres
P.O. Box 129
Big Bend National Park, TX
79834
(915) 477-2251

nomenon seen elsewhere in the park along arroyos, or washes.

On the river's gravel and sand-bars and on its cliff banks are other creatures you would not expect to find in the Chihuahuan Desert. The sandpiper and killdeer bob and sprint on the sandbars, and the cliff swallow flies up to its adobe nest fashioned of river mud.

Big Bend National Park lies in the northern third of the Chihuahuan Desert, which extends deep into Mexico. The Chihuahuan Desert, not more than 8,000 years old, is green and some-what lush, receiving most of its

rainfall during the summer months, when it is needed most. The chief plant of this desert is lechuguilla, appearing as a clump of dagger blades protruding from the desert floor. The coarse, strong fibers of the lechuguilla are used in matting, ropes, bags, and house-hold items.

Heat and seasonal winds con-tribute to the aridity of the desert. At midday in summer tempera-tures may reach 120°F, and it can be freezing cold in winter, when northern storms sweep through. But animals adapt to desert life: many beat the heat by coming out only at night, and some insects fly straight up in the air a short dis-tance, where it is significantly cooler.

The geological history of Big Bend is captured by the deep rock strata of Santa Elena, Mariscal, and Boquillas canyons. The Chisos Mountains are home to several rare species. Isolation pro-

vides the key. As the Great Ice Age drew to a close thousands of years ago, many plants and animals adapted to cooler climates became stranded in the Chisos Mountains by the lowlands' increasing aridity. The Sierra del Carmen's white-tailed deer provide a graphic example. Within the United States, these deer live only in the Chisos Mountains. Thriving on its cooler climate, junipers, Chisos oak, and pinyon pines grow in the Chisos Mountains. Mountain lion, deer, and other wildlife roam the mountains.

Big Bend National Park is rich in history. This terrain was inhabit-ed by prehistoric Native Americans at least 10,000 years ago. Since then, a variety of groups have passed through or lived on the land – Spanish explorers seek-ing gold and silver, the Apaches, the Comanches, Mexican revolu-tionaries, bandits, U.S. soldiers, farmers, and miners.

Biscayne National Park

Biscayne National Park has the simple beauty of a child's drawing. Clear blue water. Bright yellow sun. Big sky. Dark green woodlands. And here and there a boat, a bird. It is a subtropical place, where a mainland mangrove shoreline, a warm shallow bay, many small islands or keys, and living coral reefs intermingle. Together they form a vast, almost pristine wilderness and recreation area along the southeast edge of the Florida peninsula. The park, located just 21 miles east of Everglades National Park, was established as a national monument in 1968. In 1980 it was enlarged to 181,500 acres and designated a national park to protect a rare combination of terrestrial and undersea life.

Biscayne is a paradise for marine life, water birds, boaters, fishermen, snorkelers, and divers. The water is refreshingly clean and extraordinarily clear. Tropical life thrives in the region's Caribbean-like climate, saturated with year-round warmth, sunshine, and abundant rainfall. The land is filled with an unusual collection of trees, ferns, vines, flowers, and shrubs. Forests – lush, dark, humid, and ever-green – are home to many birds, butterflies, and animals.

No less diverse is Biscayne's underwater world. At its center are the coral reefs. Unlike the ocean depths, which are dark and nearly lifeless, the shallow-water reefs are light filled and burgeoning with life. Brilliantly colorful tropical fish and exotically named creatures populate the reefs – stoplight parrotfish, finger garlic sponge, goose-head scorpionfish, princess venus, peppermint goby. More than 200 types of fish can be spotted along Biscayne's reefs.

Coral reefs lie beneath clear blue water at one of Florida's natural wonders.
(NATIONAL PARK SERVICE)

Among the most puzzling creatures are the corals. Early biologists suspected they were plants. But each coral – whether brain, finger, or staghorn variety – is actually a colony of thousands of tiny, soft-bodied animals. These animals, called "polyps," are relatives of the sea anemone and jellyfish. Rarely seen in the day, the polyps emerge from their hard, stony skeletons at night to feed, catching drifting plankton in their outstretched tentacles. The coral reefs are home to a diverse population of marine creatures. Some inhabitants, like the Christmas tree worm, even live anchored to the coral. Corals are eaten by flamingo tongues, which are snail-like mollusks, and fish.

In Biscayne, the mainland mangrove shoreline has mostly been preserved. For many years, the trees of tropical or subtropical coasts were considered almost worthless. Some were cut for timber or used to make charcoal. Now the mangroves are consid-

BISCAYNE NATIONAL PARK
Established 1980
181,500 acres
P.O. Box 1369
Homestead, FL 33090
(305) 247-7275

ered vital as bird and fish habitats and as protection against the full violence of hurricanes. Mangroves have been called freaks, and a close look reveals why. Roots of the red mangrove arch stilt-like out of the water or grow down into the water from overhead branches. The roots of the black mangrove look like hundreds of cigars planted in the mud; they are breathing organs necessary for survival in this waterlogged environment.

The coastal wilderness of South Florida was the first spot in North America explored by Europeans. Spanish explorer Ponce de Leon sailed across Biscayne Bay in search of the mythical Fountain of Youth in 1513.

Biscayne Bay teems with rare wildlife. One unusual animal is the manatee. This gentle blubbery giant visits the bay in winter to graze on turtle and manatee grasses. Birds are drawn to the bay year-round. Brown pelicans patrol the surface of the bay, diving to catch their prey. White ibis travel across exposed mud flats, probing for small fish and crustaceans. Large colonies of little blue herons, snowy egrets, and other wading birds nest seasonally in the protected refuge of the Arsenicker Keys. The extremely shallow waters surrounding these mangrove islands in the south bay are especially well suited for foraging.

The Florida Keys were constructed over 100,000 years ago by billions of coral animals that created a 150-mile-long chain of underwater coral reefs. When these reefs later emerged from the sea, they became the many islands of the Florida Keys. The jungle-like forests of the Keys are populated by gumbo limbo, Jamaican dogwood, strangler fig, devil's-potato, satin-leaf, torchwood, and mahogany. These forests, called "hardwood hammocks," are refuges for zebra butterflies and rare Schaus swallowtails. Over the years, the Keys attracted, first, Native Americans and then treecutters from the Bahamas who felled massive mahoganies for shipbuilding. Early settlers on Elliott Key cleared forests and planted key limes and pineapples. Throughout the Keys subtropical forests were destroyed; Biscayne preserves some of the finest today. The islands abound with legends of pirates and buried treasure. Many shipwrecks, victims of high seas and the treacherous reefs, lie offshore.

Bryce Canyon National Park

The view from Fairyland Point. One of several trails into the fantasyland below starts here.

"Hoodoo," a synonym for "voodoo," is a fitting name for the spellbinding pillars of rock found in Bryce Canyon National Park. Paiute Indians who once lived in this region explained the colorful hoodoos as "Legend People" who were turned to stone by coyote. Today, the hoodoos have been described in various ways – named after mythical figures, as is Thor's Hammer, or after modern landscapes, as is the steep gorge known as "Wall Street."

The names of scenic areas – Fairyland Point and Rainbow Point – reflect the enchanting array of fantastic shapes in red, pink, orange, yellow, and sandstone hues that were created by millions of years of erosion. Geologists say that 10 million years ago, forces within the Earth created and then moved the massive blocks we know as the Aquarius and Paunsaugunt plateaus. Rock layers on the Aquarius now tower 2,000 feet above the same layers on the Paunsaugunt. Ancient rivers carved the tops and exposed edges of these blocks, removing some layers and sculpting intricate formations in others. The Paria Valley was created and later widened between the plateaus. These rivers shaped such striking formations as the 6-square-mile Bryce Amphitheater, the largest natural amphitheater in the park.

The Paria River and its many tributaries continue to carve the plateau edges. Rushing waters carrying dirt and gravel gully the edges and steep slopes of the Paunsaugunt Plateau, on which Bryce Canyon National Park lies. With time, tall thin ridges called "fins" emerge. Fins further erode into pinnacles and spires called "hoodoos." These, in turn, weaken and fall, adding their bright colors to the hills below.

Bryce Canyon's forests and meadows support diverse animal

life, from small mammals and birds to foxes and occasional mountain lions and black bears. Mule deer are the most common large mammal – best seen on summer mornings and evenings in roadside meadows. Mountain lions prey on mule deer in mutually beneficial population dynamics. Elk and pronghorn antelope, reintroduced nearby, are sometimes seen in the park. More than 160 species of birds visit the park yearly. In winter, mule deer, mountain lions, and coyotes migrate to lower elevations. Marmots and ground squirrels hibernate. Most bird species migrate to warmer climates, but jays, nuthatches, ravens, eagles, and owls winter here. While humans have severely reduced the habitat available to wildlife, a scarcity of water in southern Utah restricts human development, allowing for enhancement of wildlife diversity. Elevations ranging from 6,000 to 9,000 feet and diverse soil and moisture conditions influence the park's plant life. Pinyon pines and

junipers dominate lower elevations; ponderosa pines yield to spruce, fir, and aspen at higher elevations. Bristlecone pines, the park's oldest trees, grow on exposed, rocky slopes unsuitable for most other trees. More than 400 plant species – among them the gentian, bellflower, yarrow, gilia, sego lily, and manzanita – grow in the park.

Early Native Americans left lit-

**BRYCE CANYON
NATIONAL PARK
Established 1928
35,835 acres
Bryce Canyon, UT 84717
(801) 834-5322**

tle to tell us of their use of the plateaus. We know that people have been in the Colorado Plateau region for about 12,000 years, but only random fragments of worked stone tell of their presence near Bryce Canyon. Artifacts tell a more detailed story of use at lower eleva-

tions beyond the park's boundary. Both Anasazi and Fremont influences are found near the park. The people of each culture left bits of a puzzle to be pieced together by present and future archaeologists. Paiutes lived in the region when Euro-Americans arrived in southern Utah.

The Paiutes were living throughout the area when Captain Clarence E. Dutton explored here with Major John Wesley Powell in the 1870s. Many of today's place-names come from this time. Dutton's report gave the name "Pink Cliffs" to the Claron Formation. Other names – Paunsaugunt, "place or home of the beavers"; Paria, "muddy water" or "elk water"; Panguitch, "water" or "fish"; and Yovimpa, "point of pines" – were derived from the Paiute language.

The Paiutes were displaced by emissaries of the Church of Christ of Latter-Day Saints, who developed the many small communities throughout Utah. Ebenezer Bryce

aided in the settlement of southwestern Utah and northern Arizona. In 1875 he came to the Paria Valley to live and harvest timber from the plateau. Neighbors called the canyon behind his home "Bryce's Canyon." Today it remains the name not only of one canyon but also of a national park.

Shortly after 1900, visitors were coming to see the colorful geologic sights, and the first accommodations were built along the Paunsaugunt Plateau rim, above Bryce's Canyon. By 1920, efforts were started to set aside these scenic wonders. In 1923, President Warren G. Harding proclaimed part of the area as Bryce Canyon National Monument under the Powell (now Dixie) National Forest. In 1924, legislation was passed to establish the area as Utah National Park, but the provisions of this legislation were not met until 1928. Legislation was passed that year to change the name of the new park to Bryce Canyon National Park.

Carved from the Pink Cliffs, 50- to 60-million-year-old lake deposits, the Bryce Amphitheater is one of the most distinctive landscapes in the world.

Part of the Wall of Windows, seen from the Peekaboo Loop Trail below Bryce Point.

Canyonlands National Park

Last light from the sun on Junction Butte, seen from Grand View Point, Island in the Sky district.

Canyonlands preserves an immense wilderness of rock at the heart of the Colorado Plateau. Water and gravity have been the prime architects of this land, cutting flat layers of sedimentary rock into hundreds of colorful canyons, mesas, buttes, fins, arches, and spires. At center stage are two great canyons, those carved by the Green and Colorado rivers.

Surrounding the rivers are vast, and very different, regions of the park: to the north, Island in the Sky; to the west, The Maze; and to the east, The Needles. The areas share a common primitive spirit and wild desert atmosphere. Each also offers its own special rewards. Few people were familiar with these remote lands and rivers when the park was established in

1964. Indigenous peoples, cowboys, river explorers, and uranium prospectors had dared to enter this rugged corner of southeastern Utah, but few others did. To a large degree, Canyonlands remains unspoiled today. Its roads are mostly unpaved, its trails primitive, its rivers free-flowing. Throughout the park roam desert bighorn sheep, coyotes, and other animals native to this land. Canyonlands is wild America.

Views from the Island in the Sky stretch across canyons to the horizon 100 miles distant. A broad, level mesa wedged between the Green and Colorado, Island in the Sky serves as Canyonlands' observation tower. Closest to the mesa's edge is the White Rim, a nearly continuous sandstone bench 1,200 feet below the Island. Another 1,000 feet beneath the White Rim are the rivers, shadowed by sheer canyon cliffs, and beyond them lies the country of The Maze and The Needles.

Outside the park's boundary,

three jagged mountain ranges abruptly break the pattern of the flat-topped canyon landscape. To the east rise the La Sals; to the south, the Abajos; to the southwest, the Henrys. Rain that passes by the arid soil of Canyonlands keeps these mountains mantled in forests of pine and fir. On the Island, vegetation is much sparser. Open fields of Indian rice grass and other grasses and pinyon–juniper pygmy forests survive on less than 10 inches of rain a year. Coyotes, foxes, squirrels, ravens, hawks, and smaller birds share the food of these lands. Rocky ledges that lead down to and below the White Rim are a favorite habitat for many of Canyonlands' desert bighorn sheep.

The many trails around Island in the Sky lead to striking vistas, arches, and other outstanding geological features. Geologists would probably single out Upheaval Dome as the oddest geologic feature on Island in the Sky. Measuring 1,500 feet deep, the Dome does not look like a

**CANYONLANDS
NATIONAL PARK**
Established 1964
337,570 acres
125 West 200 South
Moab, UT 84532
(801) 259-7164

dome at all, but rather like a crater. One popular theory suggests that Upheaval Dome was created by slow-moving underground salt deposits that pushed layers of sandstone upward. Another more recent theory suggests that the Dome was created when a meteor hit.

The Maze country west of the Colorado and Green rivers is Canyonlands at its wildest. It ranks as one of the remotest and least accessible sections in the United States. There is The Maze itself, a perplexing jumble of canyons, that has been described as a "30-square-mile puzzle in sandstone." Beyond are the weirdly shaped towers, walls, buttes, and mesas of the Land of Standing Rocks, Ernies Country, The Doll House, and The Fins.

Until the park was created, few individuals had explored these canyons. Even today there are few visitors. Many of them come to see the ghostly figures painted on the walls of Horseshoe Canyon, which were left by Indians at least 2,000 years ago. The haunting lifesize forms are considered among the finest examples of prehistoric rock art in the country.

The contrasting names in The Needles country reflect the diversity of the land itself: Devils Kitchen and Angel Arch, Elephant Hill and Caterpillar Arch, Gothic Arch and Paul Bunyans Potty. The Needles is a startling landscape of sculptured rock spires, arches, canyons, grabens, and potholes. The dominant landforms are The Needles themselves – rock pinnacles banded in red and white. Earth movements fractured the rock, and water, wind, and freezing and thawing eroded it into the jumbled terrain of today. Grassy meadows such as the 960-acre Chesler Park offer a striking contrast to The Needles' bare rock. And arches add a touch of the unusual to the region. Like Arches National Park to the northeast, The Needles

country boasts a fascinating collection of natural rock spans. Angel Arch, located in a side canyon of Salt Creek Canyon, stands 150 feet high. The Wooden Shoe Arch, on the other hand, has just a small tunnel-like opening. Other arches are shaped like a caterpillar, a wedding ring, and a horse's hoof. Throughout this country the Anasazi Indians – the Ancient ones – once ranged.

The Green and Colorado rivers – the only major source of

water in the midst of a dry expanse – attract a variety of wildlife. Deer, fox, beaver, bobcats, and migratory birds find shelter in the riverside cottonwoods, tamarisks, and willows. Hanging gardens of lush maidenhair fern, monkeyflower, and columbine cling to the 1,200-foot-high cliffs along water-seepage lines. As in other corners of the park, cliffside stone houses and rock art of ancient Indians are scattered along the rivers.

An approaching thunderstorm blackens the sky behind The Fins in Ernies Country.

Capitol Reef National Park

A giant, sinuous wrinkle in the Earth's crust stretches for 100 miles across south-central Utah. This impressive buckling of rock, created by the same tremendous forces that built the Colorado Plateau 65 million years ago, is called "the Waterpocket Fold." Capitol Reef National Park preserves the Fold and its spectacular, eroded jumble of colorful cliffs, massive domes, soaring spires, stark monoliths, twisting canyons, and graceful arches. But the Waterpocket Fold country is more than this. It is also the free-flowing Fremont River and the big desert sky. It is cactus, jay, lizard, jackrabbit, juniper, columbine, and deer. It is a place where Indians hunted and farmed for more than 1,000 years and, later, where Mormon pioneers settled to raise their families. It is the inspiration for poets, artists, and photographers.

The Waterpocket Fold country can be explored fleetingly along Utah Highway 24, the major east–west highway through the

The white rock domes and cliffs of Capitol Reef rise above the Fremont River in the center of the park.

park, and on the Scenic Drive, a gravel road that provides a 25-mile round-trip tour of the park. Utah Highway 24, built in 1962, follows the serpentine Fremont River as it winds its way through the Fold. Above the road tower the brilliantly colored cliffs and domes of Capitol Reef, the park's namesake. This especially majestic part of the Waterpocket Fold is named for its vaulted white rock domes and its nearly impassable ridges (pioneers sometimes called these ridges "reefs"). The Scenic Drive follows the west face of the Fold and leads into Grand Wash and Capitol Gorge, two deep, twisting, water-carved, sheer-walled canyons. Along the Scenic Drive are trails that lead to overlooks, remote canyons, natural arches, and slick-rock wilderness.

Life in the Waterpocket Fold country is most abundant along the Fremont River. Native Americans, early pioneers, moisture-loving plants, and many animals have found refuge near its waters.

People of the little-known but widespread "Fremont Culture" lived along the river as early as A.D. 700, sharing the rugged slick-rock wilderness of the Colorado Plateau with the Anasazi, who lived to the south. The Fremont people hunted and gathered their food, and grew corn, beans, and squash as well. When they mysteriously disappeared sometime after A.D. 1250, they left behind few traces of their life here. The rock art they painted (pictographs) on and incised (petroglyphs) into canyon walls can still be seen in several places. Later, nomadic Utes and Paiutes hunted throughout the Waterpocket Fold country.

Explorers, Mormon pioneers,

and others began to make their way into the valley of the Fremont River in the late 1800s. Settling beyond the valley required a trip across the rough terrain of the Waterpocket Fold. A narrow, rocky travel route that cut through the Fold was Capitol Gorge. One rock wall, called "the Pioneer Register," is filled with the names of miners, settlers, and others who passed through this canyon beginning in 1871. By 1917, the tiny Mormon community of Fruita was bustling on the banks of the Fremont. With skillful irrigation of the good soil of the valley, Fruita became well known for its productive orchards and the quality of its fruit. Flooding sometimes occurred, but the town was spared any serious destruction. After Capitol Reef National Monument (later to become Capitol Reef National Park) was set aside in 1937, the farmers and their families gradually moved away. The heritage of these pioneers is preserved in an old log schoolhouse, where socials, dances, and church meetings were once held, and in other structures scattered around the still-thriving historic orchards and fields of Fruita.

Today, the life along the Fremont River consists of the life of cottonwoods, willows, and ash, which create a fresh ribbon of green each spring, and of Indian paintbrush, goldenpea, and other seasonal wildflowers. It is the life of animals drawn by the magnet of water: birds galore, from mountain bluebirds to migratory ducks, and mammals, from marmots to mule deer. But move away from the river – even just a few hundred yards – and the harsh, sparser environment of the desert dominates.

Miles of unpaved roads lead into remote areas of the Waterpocket Fold country, once of interest only to cowboys, geologists, miners, and sheepherders. Today, these areas offer natural beauty and solitude to park visitors. In vast expanses such as Cathedral Valley, golden eagles soar and solitary stone monoliths tower over sandy desert plains. In secluded canyons such as Halls Creek Canyon, hanging gardens of monkeyflower and maidenhair fern grace canyon walls. Many roads, such as Burr Trail, offer panoramic views that are increasingly breathtaking as they climb to the top of the Waterpocket Fold.

CAPITOL REEF NATIONAL PARK
Established 1971
241,904 acres
HC 70, Box 15
Torrey, UT 84775
(801) 425-3791

In the back country the desert dominates, and it stands in stark contrast to the Fremont River valley, a rare oasis. Less than 8 inches of rain fall per year, most of it in late-summer thunderstorms. These storms can turn dry, sandy washes into raging torrents, threatening some forms of life and sustaining others. Twisted, stunted juniper and pinyon pine, which dot the landscape along with other hardy plants, are testimony to the severity of the desert. But many plants and animals are well adapted for life here. In different ways, kangaroo rats, lizards, cactuses, and saltbush cope with the perennial water shortage of the desert. Some are experts at collecting and storing water; others, at water conservation; some, at both. Many animals move about only at night to escape the heat of day, so the

casual observer can easily underestimate the richness of animal life in the desert.

Occasionally, pools of rainwater collect in eroded bowl-like depressions in the rock called "waterpockets." Oddly, the tiny waterpocket is the namesake of the massive Fold that dominates this landscape. Bighorn sheep and bobcats – and even people – have quenched their thirst at these holes.

Flowers at the base of pocked cliffs along Grand Wash.

Carlsbad Caverns National Park

Away from the sunlight, the flowering cactus of the Chihuahuan Desert, the rugged mountain range of the Guadalupes, the songs of the desert birds, and the howl of the coyote lies the celebrated underground world of New Mexico's Carlsbad Caverns. It is an incomparable realm of gigantic subterranean chambers, fantastic cave formations, and extraordinary features. The park contains eighty separate caves, including the deepest in the United States, at 1,593 feet, and the fourth longest.

Altogether more than 20 miles of Carlsbad Caverns have been discovered, and the cave formations are still being explored by speleologists, or cave scientists. Spelunkers can visit three of these miles along paved and well-lighted trails, choosing between the Blue Tour (a 3-mile, 2 ½- to 3-hour walk) and the Red Tour (a 1 ¼-mile, 1- to 1 ½-hour walk).

On the Blue Tour, visitors can

Stalactites hang from the ceiling in the Big Room.

see all of the chambers open to the public – the Main Corridor, the Scenic Rooms, and the Big Room. The Main Corridor is not greatly decorated with cave formations, but its size – more than ¼-mile long with ceiling heights of more than 200 feet – is impressive. Equally impressive is the depth to which it takes you – 829 feet below the Earth's surface. The scattered decorations in the Main Corridor include stalactites, stalagmites, and flowstone. At the end of the Main Corridor lies Iceberg Rock, a 200,000-ton boulder that fell from the ceiling thousands of years ago. The Main Corridor leads into the smaller Scenic Rooms. The first is the Green Lake Room, a wonderland of thousands of delicate stalactites, marble-like flowstone, and 8-foot-deep Green Lake. Past the rest of the exquisitely decorated Scenic Rooms – the Kings Palace, the Queens Chamber, and the Papoose Room – is the Boneyard, an undecorated area that may resemble what

CARLSBAD CAVERNS NATIONAL PARK

Established 1930

46,766 acres

3225 National Parks Highway

Carlsbad, NM 88220

(505) 785-2232

Carlsbad Caverns looked like during the early years of formation.

The Red Tour explores the immense subterranean chamber called, appropriately, "the Big Room." Cross-shaped, it measures 1,800 feet at its longest, 1,100 feet at its widest, and 255 feet at its highest. Located 755 feet down, it is one of the largest underground chambers in the world. This "room" is resplendent with cave formations, including the 62-foot-high Giant Dome, Carlsbad's biggest stalagmite, and the 42-foot-high Twin Domes in the Hall of Giants, as well as numerous other stalagmites, stalactites, columns, draperies, and flowstone formations. Some other highlights of the tour are crystal-clear Mirror Lake, and the Bottomless Pit, a black hole 140 feet deep.

Visitors seeking a more rugged tour can explore New Cave, an underground wilderness without electricity, paved walkways, or other modern conveniences. Among the highlights of this 2-hour, 1 ¼-mile tour are the 89-foot-high Monarch, one of the world's tallest columns; the sparkling, crystal-decorated Christmas Tree column; and the Chinese Wall, a delicate, ankle-high rimstone dam.

The creation of Carlsbad Caverns began 250 million years ago from a reef in an inland sea. Cracks developed in the reef as it grew seaward. Eventually the sea evaporated and the reef was buried under deposits of salts and gypsum. Then, a few million years ago, uplift and erosion began to uncover the buried rock reef. Slightly acidic water began dissolving the limestone and forming the large underground chambers of the cavern. The exposed reef became part of the Guadalupes, and the underground chambers became Carlsbad Caverns.

The decoration of its caverns with stalactites, stalagmites, and other formations began more than

500,000 years ago. Cave formations developed slowly, created by drops of water carrying small amounts of dissolved limestone. The glistening formations were formed by the tiny quantities of minerals deposited by the raindrops seeping into the cave. Billions of drops later, thousands of cave formations had taken shape.

The evening flight of the bats is a natural phenomenon as fascinating as the rare cave formations. Carlsbad Caverns is a sanctuary for about 300,000 Mexican free-

tailed bats, which, during the day, crowd together on the ceiling of Bat Cave, a passageway near the entrance. In a mass exodus at dusk, thousands of bats fly from the cave for a night of feasting on moths and other insects. Silhouetted against the night sky like a dark, swift-moving cloud, the dramatic spectacle of the bats can be viewed from the outdoor amphitheater at the cave's natural entrance. Because the bats winter in Mexico, the flights occur only from early spring through October.

Drapery-like formations hang near the entrance to the Main Corridor.

Channel Islands National Park

The Channel Islands, an island chain lying just off California's southern coast, and the surrounding seas provide an important breeding ground for seabirds; a protected habitat for whales, seals, sea lions, and other marine animals; and receptive ground for plants, some of which grow only on these islands. Five of the eight islands and their surrounding 1 nautical mile of ocean, with its massive kelp forests, compose Channel Islands National Park. In 1980, Congress designated Anacapa, Santa Cruz, Santa Rosa, San Miguel, and Santa Barbara Islands, and 125,000 acres of submerged lands, as a national park because they possess outstanding and unique natural and cultural resources. Later that year the ocean 6 miles out around each island was designated as a national marine sanctuary. The park provides habitat for marine life ranging from microscopic plankton to Earth's largest mammal, the blue whale, and protection from such human

The Channel Islands off southern California's coast provide important sanctuaries for a range of wildlife. (DAVID MUENCH)

encroachments as offshore oil rigs.

For many plants and animals of the Channel Islands, life is dependent on both land and sea. Pelicans fish for anchovies from the ocean but nest on the dry bluffs of West Anacapa. Low-growing sand verbena needs the sandy soil of San Miguel Island to grow, but to thrive it also needs salt

from the ocean air. Giant kelp fastens its root-like hold-fasts on the shallow rocks of islands' nearshore reefs, yet this seaweed also needs the nutrients from the deep ocean.

Isolation from the mainland and the mingling of warm- and cold-water currents in the Santa Barbara Channel help form the Channel Islands' unique character.

The plants and animals are similar to those on the mainland, but thousands of years of isolation in these island environments have resulted in size, shape, or color variations among some plants and animals. All of the larger islands are home to the island fox, a close relative of the mainland's gray fox. But because it evolved in isolation, the island fox is no larger than a house cat. These foxes prey upon deer mice that are slightly larger than their mainland relatives. Both creatures are well adapted to the harsh island environment.

Remoteness from the mainland has buffered the islands from the rapid changes wrought by modern man. While most mainland tidepools are practically devoid of life because of heavy human use, abalone, sea urchins, sea anemones, and limpets thrive in the islands' intertidal areas. White-plumed sea anemones still cover underwater rocks at San Miguel, and vivid purple hydrocorals filter water for food near Santa Cruz Island. Though used by fishermen and sport divers, and subject to mainland water pollutants, the kelp forests of the Channel Islands harbor great numbers of plants and animals.

The Channel Islands have not only diverse wildlife but also a rich cultural heritage. More than 180 largely undisturbed archaeological sites have been mapped beneath Santa Rosa. These include several associated with early man's presence in North America, such as Chumash Indian villages and historic-era camps of early explorers and fur hunters. The Chumash, or "island people," had villages on the northern islands and traded with the mainland Indians. The southern island of Santa Barbara was home to the Gabrielino people. In 1542, explorer Juan Rodriquez Cabrillo entered the Santa Barbara Channel. Cabrillo, believed to be a Portuguese navigator in service to

Spain, was the first European to land on the islands. While on his northbound odyssey of discovery, Cabrillo wintered on an island he called "San Lucas" (San Miguel or possibly Santa Rosa Island). He died as a result of a fall suffered on

CHANNEL ISLANDS NATIONAL PARK
Established 1980
249,354 acres
1901 Spinnaker Drive
Ventura, CA 93001
(805) 658-5730

that island and is believed to have been buried on one of the Channel Islands, although his grave has never been found. Subsequent explorers included Sebastian Vizcaino, Gaspar de Portola, and English captain George Vancouver,

who, in 1793, fixed the present names of the islands on nautical charts. Beginning in the late 1700s, and on into the 1800s, Russian, British, and American fur traders searched the islands' coves and shorelines for sea otter. Because its fur was highly valued, the otter was hunted almost to extinction. Hunters then concentrated on taking seals and sea lions for the fur and oil. Several of these species faced extinction as well. In the early 1800s the Chumash and Gabrielino people were removed to the mainland missions. Hunters, settlers, and ranchers soon came to the islands. By the mid-1800s, except for the fishing, based in cove camps, ranching was the economic mainstay. The Santa Cruz Island ranch produced sheep, cattle, honey, olives, and some of the finest early California wines. In the late 1800s, the ranch on Santa Rosa

Island was a major supplier of sheep to Santa Barbara and Los Angeles County markets. Anacapa, San Miguel, and Santa Barbara islands also were heavily grazed or cultivated. In the early 1900s, the U.S. Lighthouse Service – later the U.S. Coast Guard – began its stay on Anacapa Island. The U.S. Navy assumed control of San Miguel Island just before the Second World War. The islands served an important role in southern California's coastal defenses. The military's presence on San Miguel, Santa Rosa, and the other Channel Islands is evident even today.

A series of federal and landowner actions have helped preserve these nationally significant island treasures. And Channel Islands National Park is part of the international Man and the Biosphere program to conserve genetic diversity.

Crater Lake National Park

On sunny summer days, neither words nor photographs can capture Crater Lake's remarkable deep-blue brilliance. This jewel of the Cascade Range is surrounded by rolling mountains, volcanic peaks, and evergreen forests. Crater Lake lies within the caldera of Mount Mazama, a dormant volcano of the Cascade Range, which extends from Canada's Mount Garibaldi to Lassen Peak in northern California.

This stunning landscape was constructed in recent geologic time by natural forces. Lava flows first formed a high plateau base on which explosive eruptions then built the Cascade volcanoes during the past 750,000 years. For half a million years, Mount Mazama produced massive eruptions, interrupting long periods of quiet. Ash, cinders, and pumice exploded upward, building the mountain to a height of about 12,000 feet. Parasitic cones on Mazama's flanks created Mount Scott and Hillman

Surrounded by a rim that rises as much as 2,000 feet above the water, Crater Lake is much larger than it appears to the naked eye.

Peak. Glaciers periodically covered Mount Mazama's flanks and carved out the U-shaped valleys such as Munson Valley and Kerr Notch. About 6,850 years ago, the climactic eruptions of Mount Mazama

**CRATER LAKE
NATIONAL PARK
Established 1902
183,227 acres
P.O. Box 7
Crater Lake, OR 97604
(503) 594-2211**

occurred. Ash from these eruptions lies scattered over eight states and three Canadian provinces; some 5,000 square miles were covered with 6 inches of Mazama's ash. In the park's Pumice Desert, the ash is 50 feet deep. The eruptions were forty-two times greater than those of Mount St. Helens in 1980. The Mazama magma chamber was emptied and the volcano collapsed, leaving a huge bowl-shaped caldera. The high mountain was gone. At first the caldera's floor was

too hot to hold water. Renewed volcanism sealed the caldera and built the Wizard Island and Merriam cones, volcanoes within a volcano.

As volcanic activity subsided, water began to collect. For the past 4,000 years, the volcano has not stirred. Springs, snow, and rain began to fill the caldera until it became, at a depth of 1,932 feet, the deepest lake in the United States.

Humans probably witnessed the cataclysmic eruption of Mount Mazama. Shamans in historic time forbade most Indians to view the lake, and Indians said nothing about it to trappers and pioneers, who for fifty years did not find it. Then, in 1853, while searching for the Lost Cabin Gold Mine, some prospectors, including John Wesley Hillman, happened on Crater Lake.

Crater Lake got its name in 1869 from James Sutton, editor of the *Oregon Sentinel* of Jacksonville, Oregon. He named it after the small crater at the top of Wizard Island, the cinder cone in the lake that rises some 760 feet above the water. The lake was established as a national park in 1902 after sev-

enteen years of lobbying by William Gladstone Steel, who had learned of Crater Lake as a Kansas schoolboy reading a newspaper used to wrap his lunch.

For much of the year – usually October to July at higher elevations – a thick blanket of snow encircles the lake. Snowfall provides most of the park's annual 69 inches of precipitation. Crater Lake rarely freezes over; it last did in 1949. Heat from the summer sun stored in the immense body of water retards ice formation throughout the winter.

The clean, clear, cold lake water contained no fish until they were introduced by humans from 1888 to 1941. Today, rainbow trout and kokanee salmon still survive in Crater Lake. Wildflowers bloom late and disappear early here, thriving in wet, open areas. Birds and other animals often seen are ravens, jays, nutcrackers, deer, ground squirrels, and chipmunks. Present but seldom seen are elk, black bears, foxes, porcupines, pine martens, chickaree squirrels, and pikas.

Death Valley National Park

A bush has gained a rare roothold amid the sand dunes of Mesquite Flat.

Death Valley. The name is forbidding. Yet in this valley, or its surrounding mountains, is a spectacular display of wildflowers, snow-covered peaks, beautiful multicolored sand dunes, abandoned mines, and the hottest spot (over 130°F) in North America. The park, much of which lies below sea level, also boasts the lowest point in the Western Hemisphere – 282 feet below sea level. This unique landscape, which extends from eastern California to southern Nevada, has been designated part of the Mojave and Colorado Deserts Biosphere Reserve, and in 1994 was upgraded in status from a national monument to a national park.

On any given day, this valley floor shimmers silently in the heat. The air is clear – so much so that distances are telescoped – and the sky, except perhaps for a wisp of cloud, is a deep blue. For six months of the year, unmerciful heat dominates this scene, and for the next six the heat releases its grip only slightly. Rain rarely gets past the guardian mountains. The little that falls, however, is the life force of the wildflowers that transform this desert into a vast garden.

Despite the harshness and severity of the environment, more than 900 kinds of plants live within the park. Those on the valley floor have adapted to desert life by a variety of means. Some have roots that extend to a depth that is ten times the height of an average person. Some plants have a root system that lies just below the surface but sprawls extensively in all directions. Others have skins that allow very little evaporation. Different forms of wildlife, too, have learned to cope with this heat. The animals that live in the desert are mainly nocturnal; once the sun sets, the temperature falls quickly because of the dry air. Night, the time of seeming vast emptiness, is the time of innumerable comings and goings by little animals. Larger animals, such as the desert bighorn, live in the cooler, higher elevations. With height, moisture increases, too, until on the high peaks there are forests of

**DEATH VALLEY
NATIONAL PARK**
Established 1994
2,067,628 acres
P.O. Box 579
Death Valley, CA 92328
(Also in Nevada)
(619) 786-2331

juniper, mountain mahogany, and pinyon and other pines. And often the peaks surrounding the valley are snow-covered.

Death Valley's size and the distances between its major features make the use of an automobile essential. The approach to the park from the south is via California Highway 127. From Shoshone, California, to Furnace Creek is 69 miles. In a wet spring, wildflower displays in Jubilee Pass are stunning. Farther on, you pass the ruins of Ashford Mill, which was built to process gold ore. Turning northward, the road skirts the edge of the Death Valley Salt Pan. The road goes below sea level shortly

before reaching Ashford Mill and stays below all the way to Furnace Creek. In fact, it goes as low as 282 feet below sea level near Badwater. North of Badwater, a short dirt spur road leads to Devil's Golf Course. Here the Salt Pan surface is covered with jagged rock-salt spikes. A bit farther, on the east side of the main road, is Artists Drive, a loop through colorful badlands and canyon country. From the vicinity of the Furnace Creek Visitor Center, a road leads 24 miles through the badlands landscape of Furnace Creek Wash to Dantes View. From the overlook at Dantes View, you can see the lowest point in the Western Hemisphere, plus spectacular views of the Panamint Range and the surrounding mountains. On clear winter days it is even possible to see 14,375-foot Mount Williamson in the Sierra Nevadas.

In the northern part of the park are Ubehebe Crater and Scottys Castle. Ubehebe Crater, 2,400 feet in diameter, was created about 1,000 years ago during a tremen-

dously destructive volcanic eruption. Eight miles away, in Grapevine Canyon, is Scottys Castle, the grandiose home of a famous prospector.

From Emigrant Canyon Road on the west side of the park, you can reach Wildrose Canyon, where you will find a row of abandoned charcoal kilns. These kilns were constructed more than a century ago to manufacture charcoal for use in ore smelters from the surrounding pinyon-pine and juniper forest. Chinese laborers built the kilns without mortar, and Shoshone Indians tended them.

A few points of interest are easily accessible on foot. The Harmony Borax Works lies about 350 yards north of the campgrounds at Furnace Creek. Harmony dates from 1883 and was the first successful borax plant in Death Valley. Visitors can also hike to the Sand Dunes or Golden or Mosaic canyons, or climb up a 7-mile trail to the top of Telescope Peak, the highest spot in Death Valley.

ABOVE: Rays of the late-afternoon sun fan across the view from Zabrieski Point.

LEFT: As if making up for the rest of the park's exceptional barrenness, the land along Artists Drive displays a geology of varied and vivid color.

Denali National Park and Preserve

Bearberry leaves in bright autumn color carpet the tundra above the McKinley River.

Nearby Athabascan Native peoples called Mount McKinley, North America's highest mountain, Denali, or the "High One." The 20,320-foot mountain reigns in lofty isolation over the Alaska Range, that magnificent 600-mile arc of mountains that divides south-central Alaska from the interior plateau. Larger than Massachusetts, at more than 6 million acres, the park exemplifies interior Alaska's character as one of the world's last great frontiers of wilderness. The glaciers, lakes, forests, tundra, and flora and fauna are largely unspoiled, as the Athabascans knew them.

Paradoxically, this expansive landscape, habitat of large caribou, moose, and grizzly bear, lies adorned with tiny plants. Their diminutive beauty contrasts with their large importance as food to the animals that live or migrate through here.

Spring, summer, and fall provide a compressed respite from the subarctic's long season of deep cold. For most animals it is a busy period, as they must garner most of their annual food supplies. Dall's sheep, relatives of the bighorn, graze the alpine tundra for the young shoots of mountain avens. Ewes and rams live apart in summer, while the lambs are getting their start. In early summer, sheep are at lower elevations, but they will follow the snowmelt higher and higher as summer progresses.

Caribou, like the Dall's sheep, travel in groups. Both sexes sport antlers, the only deer-family members to do so. Caribou migrate great distances from their calving grounds south of the Alaska Range and northwest of Mount McKinley to their winter range in the northern reaches of the park and preserve. The Denali herd has fluctuated greatly in number over the last thirty years. Today a group of fifty or more may be seen from the park road, quite different from the thousands seen many years ago. Moose, the deer family's largest members, are not herd animals. Bulls may group in threes or fours or wander alone until they pursue several cow moose during the rut, or mating season. Wolves are rarely seen, but they play an important role in the natural scheme. In winter, wolves generally hunt in packs. However, individuals are seen as well.

Grizzly bears are omnivores, eating small plants, berries, ground squirrels, moose or caribou calves, and occasional carrion. They are seen throughout the park. Wolves and grizzly bears play an important role as predators. Ever ready to take advantage of an opportunity, they cull old, newborn, and sick animals from the caribou, moose, and sheep populations.

DENALI NATIONAL PARK AND PRESERVE
Established 1917
National park: 5,000,000 acres; National preserve: 1,500,000 acres
P.O. Box 9
McKinley Park, AK 99755
(907) 683-2294

Smaller mammals abound within the limits of this harsh, northern environment: fox, weasel, wolverine, lynx, marten, snowshoe hare, hoary marmot, red squirrel, ground squirrel, pika, porcupine, beaver, shrew, vole, and lemming. Thirty-seven mammal species have been recorded in the park and preserve.

Birdlife is varied and interesting. Raven, ptarmigan, magpie, and gray jay are some of the species that winter here. Most birds migrate long distances between their nesting grounds here in the park and their wintering areas. Wheatears winter in Africa, arctic terns in Antarctica and southern South America, and jaegers take to life at sea in the southern oceans. On the open tundra, you may easily see ptarmigan, Lapland longspurs, and various shorebirds. Short-eared owls and northern harriers can be seen soaring low in search of rodents. Golden eagles patrol the higher elevations and ridgetops. Raptors, birds of prey, of the spruce forest are the hawk owl and goshawk. In these forests, you may also see the spruce grouse and varied thrush. Plovers, gyrfalcons, mew gulls, and snow buntings are among the 159 species of birds recorded here.

This wildlife sanctuary was inhabited by generations of native Athabascans before Europeans began to explore it. Nomadic bands hunted throughout the lowland hills of Denali's northern reaches, spring through fall, for caribou, sheep, and moose.

The park, originally named "Mount McKinley National Park," was established in 1917 to protect its large mammals, and not to honor majestic Mount McKinley. Charles Sheldon, a naturalist, hunter, and conservationist, conceived the plan to conserve the region as a national park. Its populations of Dall's sheep and other wildlife were now legislatively protected. However, Mount McKinley itself was not wholly included within the boundaries.

Sheldon wanted to call the park "Denali," but his suggestion would not be followed until 1980. That year the boundary was expanded to include both the Denali caribou herd's wintering and calving grounds and the entire Mount McKinley massif. More than tripled in size, the park became Denali National Park and Preserve. Mount McKinley remains named for former senator – and later, president – William McKinley. The park was also designated an International Biosphere Reserve, significant for its potential for subarctic ecosystems research.

ABOVE: Denali (Mount McKinley) in the late afternoon. No mountain on earth rises higher above its own snowline, the lowest limit of permanent ice and snow.

RIGHT: Almost dwarfed by the immensity of nearby Mount McKinley, these other peaks of the Alaska Range are nevertheless spectacular, rising two vertical miles above their surroundings.

Dry Tortugas National Park

Almost 70 miles west of Key West, Florida, lies a cluster of seven islands composed of coral reefs and sand, called "the Dry Tortugas." With the surrounding shoals and turquoise water, they make up Dry Tortugas National Park, an area known for its bird and marine life and pirate legends.

Fort Jefferson, its central cultural feature, is the largest nineteenth-century American coastal fort. First named *Las Tortugas*, "The Turtles," by Spaniard Ponce de Leon in 1513, these reefs soon read "Dry Tortugas" on mariners' charts to show they had no fresh water. In 1825 a lighthouse was built on Garden Key to warn sailors of rocky shoals; in 1856 the present light on Loggerhead Key was built. By 1829 the United States knew it could control navigation to the Gulf of Mexico and protect Atlantic-bound Mississippi River trade by fortifying the Tortugas. Fort Jefferson's construction began on Garden Key in 1846 and con-

tinued for thirty years but never was finished. During the Civil War, the fort was a Union military prison for captured deserters. It also held four men convicted of complicity in President Abraham Lincoln's assassination in 1865. The army abandoned Fort Jefferson in 1874, and in 1908 the area became a wildlife refuge to protect the sooty-tern rookery from egg collectors.

Proclaimed as Fort Jefferson National Monument in 1935, the area was redesignated in 1992 as Dry Tortugas National Park to protect both the historical and the natural features. Not least among the latter are its namesakes, the endangered green sea turtle and the threatened loggerhead turtle.

Apart from touring the historic fort, snorkeling, swimming, saltwater sport fishing, and underwater photography are popular park activities. Warm, clear, and

Coral reefs shelter an abundance of fish and other sea life. (NATIONAL PARK SERVICE)

well lit, the Dry Tortugas' shallow waters foster optimal conditions for coral reefs to develop on the outer edges of tropical islands. Actual builders of these fringing reefs are small primitive animals called "polyps." Over centuries polyps accumulate in living colonies that form the reef's rigid structures so often mistaken for rocks. Though fragile, the Tortugas' reef complex supports a wealth of marine life.

Multicolored sea fans sway in gentle currents. Sea anemones thrust upward their rose and lavender tentacles in search of food. Lobsters anticipating danger wave their antennae. Sponges dot sandy bottoms, and staghorn coral clusters simulate underwater forests. Most obvious among coral-reef inhabitants are the colorful reef fish. Vivid, boldly patterned reds, yellows, greens, and blues act as camouflage, identity, warning, and courtship messages. Predatory fish include amberjacks, groupers, wahoos, tarpon, and, atop this coral-reef food pyramid, sharks and barracudas.

Hunted by humans – mostly illegally – for gourmet meat, leather, and cosmetic oils, the sea turtle has diminished greatly in numbers worldwide, but green, loggerhead, and hawksbill species are still seen in the Dry Tortugas. Sea turtles themselves prey on small marine invertebrates and forage turtle grass and other aquatic plants. Twice or more per season, females climb onto sand beaches to dig out nests, lay some hundred eggs, cover them, and retreat seaward. Hatchlings crawl seaward by instinct, but most succumb to natural predators between the nest and the sea.

In season, a continuous succession of songbirds and other migrants flies over or rests at the Dry Tortugas. Strategically set, these islands lie across a principal flyway from the United States to Cuba and South America. Familiar up north in summer, many gulls, terns, and migratory shorebirds winter here.

One great wildlife spectacle happens yearly between March

> **DRY TORTUGAS NATIONAL PARK**
> **Established 1992**
> **64,700 acres**
> **P.O. Box 6208**
> **Key West, FL 33041**
> **(305) 242-7700**

and September as some 100,000 sooty terns gather on Bush Key for their nesting season. They come from the Caribbean Sea and west-central Atlantic Ocean. As early as mid-January, sooties perform nocturnal maneuvers above the Dry Tortugas but spend their days at sea. When they do land here in February, egg-laying starts immediately. Bush Key is closed to landings during tern nesting season, but the rookery is readily observable from the fort with binoculars.

Sooty parents take turns shading from the sun their single egg, laid in a simple depression in the warm sand. Once the young grow strong enough for continuous flight, the colony disperses. Interspersed among the sooties' rookery are 2,500 breeding brown noddies. Unlike sooties and most other terns, noddies nest in vegetation, such as bay cedar and sea lavender. Both sooties and noddies feed by capturing fish and squid from the sea's surface while still in flight. Magnificent frigate birds that soar with 7-foot wingspans prey on tern hatchlings in Nature's endless give and take. Visitors often also see masked and brown boobies; roseate terns; double-crested cormorants; and brown pelicans, a species recently delisted as endangered.

Everglades National Park

Tropical life from Caribbean islands blends with temperate species in the Everglades at Florida's southernmost tip. The result is a rich mixture of plants and animals in a unique setting. This largest remaining subtropical wilderness in the coterminous United States has extensive fresh- and saltwater areas, open Everglades prairies, and mangrove forests.

"Everglades" means a marshy land covered with scattered tall grasses. A freshwater river 6 inches deep and 50 miles wide creeps seaward through the Everglades on a riverbed that slopes ever so gradually. During the wet season the water may seem to be still, but it is flowing. Along its long course, the water drops 15 feet, finally emptying into Florida Bay.

Summer's high water levels enable animals to range throughout the park. Visitors will not then see the concentrations of wildlife that are typical in winter months. Summer offers different attractions – mountainous cumulus clouds,

An example of the varied wildlife, a bird perches in a tree within Everglades National Park, high above the alligators that lie in wait below. (NATIONAL PARK SERVICE)

lush vegetation, spectacular sunsets, calm waters. It means rebirth and replenishment for the Everglades, and natural change. The violent winds and torrential rains of hurricanes may sweep northward from June to November. Visitors may see the uprooted trees and other damage suffered by the Everglades, which was ravaged by Hurricane Andrew when it swept through Florida in 1992. The Everglades winter is mild, with inclement weather rare and insects less bothersome. With winter's dry season, wildlife must congregate in and around the waterholes, many of which are visible from nature trails. Birds change their feeding habits as food grows scarce toward the end of the dry season. They leave the roadside ponds they frequent early in the season, moving northward to more plentiful food supplies.

The Everglades is best known for its abundance and variety of birdlife. At Flamingo, visitors may be able to watch roseate spoonbills, large pink birds often mistaken for flamingos. Reddish egrets and rare great white herons live and breed in Florida Bay. About

fifty pairs of southern bald eagles nest along the coast. Some of the endangered birds can sometimes be seen from the breezeway of the Flamingo Visitor Center. Other rare and endangered species found in the park include the Florida panther, manatee, Everglades mink, green sea turtle, loggerhead turtle, Florida sandhill crane, snail kite, short-tailed hawk, peregrine falcon, Cape Sable sparrow, and crocodile. Other species also require the special protection Everglades National Park provides. These include the alligator, reddish egret, spoonbill, Florida mangrove cuckoo, osprey, brown pelican, and round-tailed muskrat. But for this protected habitat, many would soon be threatened.

Large populations of Cape Sable sparrows once found at Cape Sable and Big Cypress are almost gone. Only widely scattered individuals remain. Taylor Slough's grass prairie supports an active population, but exotic, non-native plants threaten to close in the open prairie this sparrow needs for survival. Short-tailed hawks prey on the sparrow. When expansive habitat fostered an abundance of Cape

EVERGLADES NATIONAL PARK
Established 1947
1,506,499 acres
P.O. Box 279
Homestead, FL 33030
(305) 242-7700

Sable sparrows, this natural predation posed no great threat to the species.

Crocodiles, much less common than alligators, are distinguished by their narrower snouts and greenish gray color. These shy and secretive creatures, found only in estuaries in extreme southern Florida, particularly in northeast Florida Bay, are rarely seen. Their survival hinges on the preservation of their dwindling habitat. A crocodile sanctuary, closed to public access, has been established in Florida Bay for their protection.

The alligator is the best-known Everglades citizen. Unfortunately, its hide has been greatly prized for high-fashion shoes and accessories. The alligator once waged a losing battle against poachers and habitat loss, but it has now staged a comeback, aided by nation-wide protection. Recently, 75 percent of the nation's alligators were removed from the endangered species list and reclassified as threatened.

The alligator has earned the title "Keeper of the Everglades." It cleans out the large holes dissolved in the Everglades' limestone bed. These serve as oases in the dry winter season. Fish, turtles, snails, and other freshwater animals seek refuge in these life-rich solution holes, which become feeding grounds for alligators, birds, and mammals until the rains come. Survivors, both predators and prey, then quit the holes to repopulate the Everglades.

The Florida panther, or cougar, is among North America's rarest mammals. The major threat to the survival of these big cats is loss of the extensive habitat over which they stealthily stalk their prey. They are still seen, though rarely, in the pinelands and along the main park road.

The national park contains only part of the watery expanse for which it is named. Despite the park's size, its environment is threatened by the disruptive activities of agriculture, industry, and urban development around it. There is no guarantee that the endangered species protected in the park since its establishment in 1947 will survive. The importance and uniqueness of the Everglades ecosystem have been recognized by its designation as an International Biosphere Reserve and a World Heritage Site. But life hangs by a thread in the Everglades. Man has drastically blocked the free flow of water – the lifeblood of the Everglades – through South Florida.

Agricultural development and the continued mushrooming of metropolitan Miami demand increasing amounts of water, depleting available supplies. This, in turn, increases the threat of fire, which can destroy thin soils, inviting the invasion of exotic plants and animals that upset natural habitats. Native vegetation critical to Everglades ecology is depleted. The diversity and complexity protecting the fabric of life are diminished. The continued unchecked population growth of South Florida poses severe ecological problems. Man has irrevocably changed South Florida and altered the Everglades ecosystem.

LEFT: A heron waits for its prey.
(RALPH BRUNNER)

RIGHT: This aerial view highlights the patterns formed in the marshy grasses of the Everglades. (NATIONAL PARK SERVICE)

Gates of the Arctic National Park and Preserve

Lying entirely north of the Arctic Circle, Gates of the Arctic National Park and Preserve includes a portion of the Central Brooks Range, the northernmost extension of the Rocky Mountains. Often referred to as the greatest remaining wilderness in North America, this second-largest unit of the national park system is characterized by jagged peaks, gentle arctic valleys, wild rivers, and numerous lakes. The forested southern slopes contrast with the barren northern reaches of the site at the edge of Alaska's "north slope." The park-preserve contains the Alatna, John, Kobuk, part of the Noatak, the North Fork Koyukuk, and the Tinayguk wild rivers. And with adjacent Kobuk Valley National Park and Noatak National Preserve, it is one of the largest park areas in the world.

The dramatic title for the park – Gates of the Arctic – comes from wilderness advocate Robert Marshall, a frequent traveler in the North Fork Koyukuk drainage from 1929 to 1939. Marshall described two peaks, Frigid Crags and Boreal Mountain, as the gates from Alaska's central Brooks Range into the arctic regions of the Far North. The natural forces of wind, water, temperature, and glacial and tectonic action have sculpted a wildly varied landscape in this northernmost and east–west-trending portion of the Rocky Mountains. Southerly foothills step into waves of mountains rising to elevations of 4,000 feet. These in turn may climax in limestone or granitic peaks taller than 7,000 feet. At the Arctic Divide the ranks reverse as the tundra stretches to the Arctic Ocean. The scene is one of remote wilderness and unpopulated distances, qualities many people seek when they decide to visit Gates of the Arctic.

No trails or visitor service developments exist within the park; therefore, all visitors must be self-

High, sheer cliffs soar above a treeless cirque at the headwaters of Arrigetch Creek.

sufficient. One Nunamiut Eskimo village, Anaktuvuk Pass, lies within the park's boundaries. In the past, nomadic hunters/gatherers traveled from the forested southern slopes of the mountains of the Arctic Coast. Present-day travelers will see few signs of earlier inhabitants.

GATES OF THE ARCTIC NATIONAL PARK AND PRESERVE
Established 1980
National park: 7,523,888 acres
National preserve: 948,629 acres
P.O. Box 74680
Fairbanks, AK 99707
(907) 456-0281

Seasons are dramatic in length and levels of activity: during the short summer, plants and animals must progress rapidly through growth and reproduction cycles

before the onset of winter cold. Most activity ceases with the –20°F to –50°F temperatures that persist from November to March. In the pink, low light of the arctic winter, blue-gray shadows of opposing slopes delineate the endless white mountains. The dry climate of the interior produces little snow, but what falls endures and covers the land and rivers wrapped in ice and silence. As the low-riding sun begins its warming ascent into April's spring sky, dogsled enthusiasts occasionally may be seen in the park. Other visitors begin arriving in mid-June, although many rivers are not yet entirely free of ice. Backpacking and river trips are the predominant activities.

The park contains major portions of the range and habitat of the western arctic caribou herd. Grizzly and black bear, wolf, moose, Dall's sheep, wolverine,

and fox are also found in the park. At spring breakup, the few resident bird species are joined by migratory species from Europe, South America, Asia, tropical archipelagos, and the continental United States. Despite the variety, wildlife is widely dispersed because large areas are required to sustain life in the Arctic. Wildlife sightings may be greatly affected by the size of your party, your patterns of travel, and the weather. Sparse black-spruce forests called "taiga" – from the Russian for "land of little sticks" – dot north-facing slopes and poorly drained lowlands. Boreal forests of white spruce, aspen, and birch are typically found on south-facing slopes. Near the tree line, the shrub-thicket community of dwarf and resin birch, alder, and willow appears. Heath, moss, and fragile lichen make up the understory. Alpine

tundra communities occur in the mountainous areas and along well-drained rocky ridges. Alder thickets and tussocks often impede hiking in the Arctic. Backpackers will find both types of vegetation in valleys and on slopes.

The 1980 legislation that created Gates of the Arctic National Park and Preserve called for protection of 8.5 million acres of land. Included were mandates for ensuring that the area be managed to maintain the land's wild and undeveloped character. Far-sighted provisions also included opportunities to experience solitude, to ensure the integrity of the natural arctic environment, and to provide opportunities for wilderness recreational activities. Fish and wildlife and their habitat, cultural resources, and traditional subsistence uses were also slated for protection.

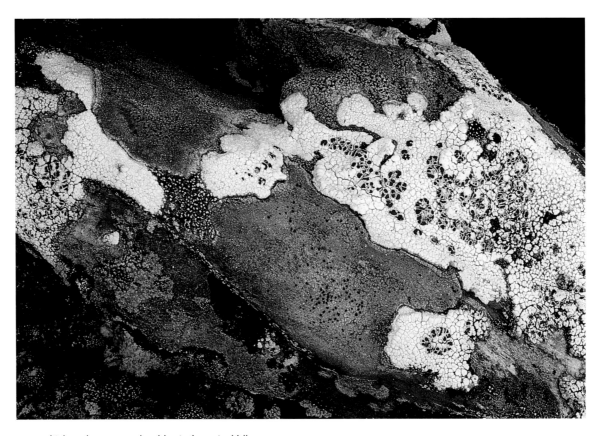

ABOVE: Lichen decorates a boulder in Aquarius Valley.

RIGHT: Some of the Arrigetch Peaks, which make up the most rugged, serrate part of the Brooks Range.

Glacier Bay National Park and Preserve

In an explosion of spray, a massive block of ice calves off the front of a tidewater glacier. (RALPH BRUNNER)

Just 200 years ago, Glacier Bay was completely covered by ice. Today, a dramatic range of plants extending from rocky terrain to lush temperate rain forest, and a large variety of wildlife, including brown and black bears, mountain goats, whales, seals, and eagles, live alongside the remaining great tidewater glaciers found in this national park and preserve.

Explorer Captain George Vancouver found Icy Strait chocked with ice in 1794, and Glacier Bay was a barely indented glacier. That glacier was more than 4,000 feet thick and up to 20 miles or more wide, and extended more than 100 miles, to the St. Elias range of mountains. But, by 1879, naturalist John Muir found that the ice had retreated 48 miles up the bay. By 1916, the Grand Pacific Glacier headed Tarr Inlet 65 miles from Glacier Bay's mouth. Such rapid retreat is known nowhere else. Scientists have documented it, hoping to learn how glacial activity relates to climate changes.

Worldwide, the glacial facts are staggering. Glaciers and polar ice store more water than lakes and rivers, groundwater, and the atmosphere combined. Ten percent of our world is under ice today, the equivalent of the percentage being farmed. If the world's ice caps thawed completely, sea level would rise enough to inundate half the world's cities. The Greenland and Antarctic ice caps are 2 miles thick. Alaska is 4 percent ice.

Glacier Bay includes sixteen tidewater glaciers, twelve of which actively calve icebergs into the bay. The show can be spectacular. As water undermines some ice fronts, great blocks of ice up to 200 feet high break loose and crash into the water. The Johns Hopkins Glacier calves such volumes of ice that it is seldom possible to approach closer than about 2 miles from its ice cliffs.

The glaciers seen here today are remnants of a general ice advance – the Little Ice Age – that began about 4,000 years ago. This advance in no way approached the extent of continental glaciation during the Pleistocene period. The Little Ice Age reached its maximum extent here about 1750, when general melting began.

GLACIER BAY NATIONAL PARK AND PRESERVE
Established 1980
National park: 3,225,284 acres
National preserve: 57,884 acres
P.O. Box 140
Gustavus, AK 99826
(907) 697-2230

The snowcapped Fairweather Range supplies ice to all glaciers on the peninsula separating Glacier Bay from the Gulf of Alaska. Mount Fairweather, the range's highest peak, stands at 15,320 feet. In Johns Hopkins Inlet, several peaks rise from sea level to 6,520 feet within just 4 miles of shore. The great glaciers of the past carved these fjords, or drowned valleys, out of the mountains like great troughs. Landslides help widen the troughs as the glaciers remove the bedrock support on upper slopes.

Huge icebergs may last a week or more. Close by, kayakers have heard the stress and strain of melting: water drips, air bubbles pop, and cracks develop. Colors betray a berg's nature or origin. White bergs hold many trapped air bubbles. Blue bergs are dense. Greenish black bergs have been calved off glacier bottoms. Dark-striped brown bergs carry morainal rubble from the joining of tributary glaciers or other sources. How high bergs – favored perches for bald eagles, cormorants, and gulls – float depends on size and ice and water density. Bergs may be weighed down, submerged even, by rock and rubble. A modest-looking berg may suddenly loom enormous, and endanger small craft, when it rolls over.

The world of science came to Glacier Bay to observe the great glaciers and found here the ideal natural laboratory for the study of the infant theory of plant succession. How do plants re-cover a raw landscape? What happens where nature wipes the slate clean and starts over from scratch? The rapid vegetation change following the glaciers' speedy retreat has enabled scientists to map and photograph the course of plant succession.

Glacier Bay has also been a site for research on whales, particularly the endangered humpback whale. Only about 7 percent of their prewhaling numbers remain. Ten species of great whales and five smaller whales swim in Alaskan waters. Glacier Bay waters boast two of the great whales, the minke and humpback, and one smaller, the orca. The whales' appeal mixes familiarity and strangeness. Whales live in family groups, aid each other in distress, and communicate with one another. The numbers of whales present can vary dramatically from year to year. Whether these variations are wholly natural or not is uncertain. Historically, most information about whales derives from attempts to harvest them, not save them from extinction.

Glacier National Park

Wildflowers thrive at the base of Florence Falls.

Precipitous peaks ranging above 10,000 feet tower over sculptured glacial valleys, ice-cold lakes that mirror mountains and sky, and alpine meadows and prairie grasslands, where wildflowers and wildlife flourish, in this exquisite park straddling the United States–Canada border.

To commemorate the long history of peace and friendship between Canada and the United States, Waterton Lakes National Park, in southwestern Alberta, and Glacier National Park, in Montana, were designated the Waterton–Glacier International Peace Park in 1932.

Wind, water, and glaciers shaped and carved this land, cutting deep U-shaped valleys and creating such stunning formations as the Garden Wall, a narrow, jagged, sharp-edged ridge, and Chief Mountain, once part of the mountains to the west, which now stands majestically alone as a result of erosion. Smaller tributary glaciers created hanging valleys. Today abundant waterfalls plunge from hanging valleys to lower elevations. While glaciers are no longer found in Waterton Lakes National Park, glaciers are still at work in the high country of Glacier National Park.

This landscape is a wilderness full of wildflowers and wildlife with distinct local variations. The high mountains that bisect the park from north to south capture rainfall on the western slopes. This warm, moist, Pacific-like environment produces dense forests of larch, spruce, fir, and lodgepole pine. In the Lake McDonald valley, forests of western red cedar and hemlock are common. The alpine areas provide the setting for some of the best wildflower displays in North America. It is a short-lived spectacle made glorious by heather, gentian, beargrass, and glacier lily. East of the divide, where the plains roll up to the mountains, pasque flower, lupine, Indian paintbrush, gaillardia, aster, and shooting star paint the prairie.

The diverse terrain supports a variety of wildlife. Bighorn sheep, mountain goats, wapiti (elk), black bear, and white-tailed deer are frequently seen. Grizzly bear, moose, wolves, and mule deer also live here year-round. Beaver, hoary marmot, river otter, marten, and pika make Waterton–Glacier their home. Locally prevalent birds include osprey, ptarmigan, golden eagle, Clark's nutcracker, and harlequin duck. The endangered bald eagle also nests and fishes here.

And Waterton Lakes National Park maintains an exhibit herd of bison in a paddock.

Though administered by separate countries and divided by the international boundary, the parks are at the same time united in the most natural of ways. Glaciers carved the Upper Waterton Valley, which lies in both nations; the native plants and animals are similar; and the massive Rocky Mountains span the two countries. Long before European explorers and settlers began to venture into the Rockies, the peoples native to this region shared the bounties of the land and considered it one.

The mid-eighteenth century brought change. The quest for furs drew trappers deep into these mountains, and boundaries were drawn, marking the domains of the great fur-trading companies of the West. Then, in 1818, the 49th parallel to the Continental Divide was established as the international boundary between the territory of the United States and what was then territory owned by Great Britain, arbitrarily dividing the natural land area of today's

Waterton–Glacier. In the late nineteenth century, farsighted men such as Frederick William Godsal in Canada and George Bird Grinnell in the United States labored to persuade their governments to set aside parts of the Rockies as wilderness recreational havens to be preserved for future generations. Their goals were reached in 1895, when Waterton Lakes National Park was established, and in 1910, when Glacier was created. As the years went by, people in both nations recognized the natural unity of the parks, and

largely through the efforts of Rotary International of Alberta and Montana, the U.S. Congress and the Canadian Parliament in 1932 established the first international peace park – Waterton–Glacier International Peace Park. Waterton Lakes and Glacier national parks have also been designated as Biosphere Reserves.

Bighorn sheep (left) and mountain goats (above) are at home in the precipitous alpine terrain of the park.

Grand Canyon National Park

The view from Point Imperial early in the morning. The prominent butte in the near distance is Mount Hayden.

Somehow "Grand" fails to capture the breathtaking immensity and beauty of this canyon. The scene continually changes as light plays off the rocks and clouds, creating shadows and contrasts. The world seems larger here, with sunrises, sunsets, and storms taking on an added dimension to match the landscape. The permutations are unceasing, as are the variations in mood. This is a land to humble the soul.

The forces of erosion created this amazing gorge. The top of the Grand Canyon stands some 8,000 feet above sea level, and sheer canyon walls plunge more than a mile down to the rapids of the Colorado River. The width of the canyon is as narrow as one-tenth of a mile from rim to rim in Marble Canyon and as broad as 18 miles farther down the river. The geological history of 2 billion years is etched into the canyon's numerous layers of rock. Geologists offer various theories as to how the Colorado River carved the canyon out of mountain ranges created by the uplifting of rock beginning an estimated 1.7 billion years ago. The cutting of the upper layers of mountains by the river, forming the distinctive buttes of the Grand Canyon, is believed to have begun between 6 and 25 million years ago. The shape of the canyon is continuously being molded by the river and the elements. The museum at Yavapai Point tells the story of the geological history of the canyon.

On a clear day, 200 miles of this solitary landscape is visible, stretching out to the horizon. The panoramic view of the canyon and Colorado River from the South Rim, which is open year-round, is the most popular, with the nearly 5 million sightseers who set foot here each year. The North Rim, which is open only from mid-May through late October, offers some relief from the crowds for those willing to travel the distance.

Although it is only 10 air miles across the canyon, the North Rim is over 200 miles away from the South Rim by car, or a 21-mile strenuous two- to three-day cross-canyon hike. The North Rim features alpine vegetation, including forests of spruce, fir, locust, ponderosa pine, and quaking aspen. Mule deer may be seen from the Cape Royal Road, which winds through scenic forests and meadows. The Kaibab Plateau of the

**GRAND CANYON
NATIONAL PARK
Established 1919
1,217,158 acres
P.O. Box 129
Grand Canyon, AZ 86023
(602) 638-7888**

North Rim is also the sole habitat of the white-tailed Kaibab squirrel.

Adventurous visitors can explore the canyon by hiking along the 8-mile Bright Angel Trail or the steeper 6 ½-mile South

Kaibab Trail to the canyon floor, where temperatures can soar to 118°F. Rafters can also experience the canyon by braving the more than 150 powerful rapids along the nearly 178 miles of the Colorado River that wind through Grand Canyon National Park. A less strenuous, though not necessarily more comfortable, means of travel is by mule. The mules follow seemingly treacherous trails on the edge of sheer cliffs. A bird's-eye view of the canyon is offered by helicopter and airplane tours from Grand Canyon Airport and Tusayan.

Visitors can get a glimpse of the past by exploring Tusayan Ruin, an excavated Anasazi pueblo dating from A.D. 1185. Nearby, the Tusayan Museum records the lives of the people who lived here before the arrival of Europeans. One of the most beautiful and remote corners of Grand Canyon, however, lies outside the park's boundary and jurisdiction. The Havasupai Indian Reservation, in a large tributary canyon on the south side of the Colorado River, is administered

by the Havasupai Indian Tribe. In the midst of this arid Arizona landscape are the clear blue waters of Havasu Creek that tumble down stunning waterfalls. The village of Supai is accessible only by an 8-mile hike or by horseback along a steep trail. Despite its remote location, Havasu Canyon draws geologists, anthropologists, botanists, and birders.

Europeans did not set foot in the Grand Canyon until 1540, when Hopi Indians brought Spaniard Don Lopez de Cardenas to the canyon. Geologist John Wesley Powell, who braved the Green and Colorado rivers in a dory in 1869, brought the wonders of the Grand Canyon to the American public. Proclaimed a national monument by President Theodore Roosevelt in 1908, Grand Canyon became a national park in 1919. The park was expanded to nearly twice its original size in 1975, and it now encompasses 1,217,158 acres of land, stretching from Glen Canyon National Recreation Area to Lake Mead National Recreation Area.

ABOVE: The morning view looking east from Yavapai Point, South Rim.

LEFT: Sunrise lights up the cliffs below Powell Point, South Rim.

Grand Teton National Park

The Grand Teton (in clouds) and the Teton Range across Jackson Lake at dawn.

The jagged peaks of the Teton Range, towering more than a mile above the valley known as Jackson Hole and rising 13,770 feet above sea level, make a spectacular skyline. No foothills obstruct this mountain range, which appears even more dramatic reflected in the large lakes at its foot.

Ancestral mountains rose here between 60 and 70 million years ago. Faults fractured these formations, and 9 million years ago today's Teton Range started rising. Glaciers shaped the Teton skyline more than any other erosional force. Sheer cirque walls, rugged ridges, and jagged peaks reflect the slow, dynamic carving by these great masses of moving ice. Glaciers also created Jackson Lake, as well as Leigh, Jenny, Taggart, Bradley, and Phelps lakes.

The Snake River, which originates in the wilderness near the south boundary of Yellowstone and meanders into Jackson Lake, provides rich habitat for a diverse array of wildlife, including herons, waterfowl, pelicans, muskrats, beavers, river otters, and moose. Slower-moving water in side channels ensures essential habitat for numerous aquatic animals and plants. Beavers, river otters, and trout swim by moose feeding on aquatic plants. Native Snake River cutthroat trout depend on the park's natural aquatic system for survival. Trout consume aquatic insects and small fish. Bald eagles, ospreys, and otters in turn feed on the trout.

Along the river, willows thrive among tall cottonwood, spruce, and occasional aspen trees. Moose browse on shrubs and trees that line the river's banks. Beavers eat the inner bark of willows, aspens, and cottonwoods, and weave branches into lodges and dams alongside channels. In the summer the river bottom teems with diving, wading, and woodland birds, while elk graze in wet meadows. During darkness, owls and other predators hunt in this riparian ecosystem.

Born of wilderness snowpack, the Snake River swells with meltwater. Trappers and settlers called it "the Mad River," as it was more than a challenge to cross during the spring. Today's challenge is to protect this powerful life-supporting river as it flows through the park and winds westward to the Pacific Ocean.

The geologic forces and natural systems that interact to produce this inspiring scenery also nurture a remarkable diversity of animals. Despite a short growing season, the Greater Yellowstone ecosystem supports the largest elk herd remaining in the world. Nearly 3,000 summer in Grand Teton. A small herd of buffalo also summers in the park and winters in the National Elk Refuge. Moose stay beside canyon streams during warm weather but seek protection from frigid winds in valley bottomlands. Seldom-seen black bears, and an occasional grizzly, forage in canyons and woodlands to store body fat for winter sleep.

Bald eagles and osprey fish and nest along the Snake River. Several eagles endure the cold months. Each spring great blue herons return to their rookeries. Trumpeter swans, the largest North American waterfowl, build sizable pond-level nests; when ice prevails they depend on warm springs in the region. Beavers dam streams to create ponds that bene-

fit Canada geese, mallards, cinnamon teals, and a multitude of summer and migratory waterfowl.

The Greater Yellowstone ecosystem, which includes the Teton Range and Jackson Hole, remains as the largest essentially intact natural area in the contiguous United States. Evergreen forests and wild rivers abound. Elk, buffalo, bears, eagles, and swans that once thrived nationwide now survive in this sanctuary.

Wildflowers in amazing variety and profusion bloom through the warm months. Sagebrush buttercups follow receding snowpack. Springbeauties, yellowbells, and steershead blossom closely behind, growing close to the ground for protection from late snowstorms or frost. Brilliant color covers the valley floor during late June, the peak of the wildflower season. Meadows of scarlet gilia,

balsamroot, lupine, larkspur, and wild buckwheat bloom in multiple combinations of red, yellow, blue, purple, and white. Following the valley display, many of the same

**GRAND TETON
NATIONAL PARK
Established 1929
309,994 acres
P.O. Box Drawer 170
Moose, WY 83012
(307) 733-2880**

wildflowers flourish in meadows along canyon trails. The alpine zone includes the official flower of the park, the alpine forget-me-not.

People entered Jackson Hole an estimated 12,000 years ago. Archaeological evidence indicates that small groups hunted and gathered plants in the valley from

5,000 to 500 years ago. During historic times no one tribe claimed ownership to Jackson Hole, but Blackfeet, Crow, Gros Ventre, Shoshone, and other Native Americans living on surrounding lands used this neutral valley during the warm months. Severe winters prevented year-round habitation.

John Colter allegedly was the first European in the valley, entering in the winter of 1807–08. Mountain men followed and trapped valley beaver. Brigades of trappers traversed this crossroads of the western fur trade until the era ended about 1840. Valley settlement began in the late 1800s, with farmers and ranchers. In 1929, much of the Teton Range received protection through the establishment of the park. After years of debate, Congress added the Jackson Hole portion in 1950.

Great Basin National Park

Great Basin National Park is a vast area of sagebrush-covered valleys and narrow mountain ranges centered on Nevada but extending into neighboring states, stretching from California's Sierra Nevada Range in the west to the Rockies of Utah in the east. The name "Great Basin" comes from a peculiarity of drainage: over most of the area, streams and rivers find no outlet to the sea. Instead, water collects in shallow salt lakes, marshes, and mud flats, where it evaporates in the dry desert air. There is not just one basin here but many, all separated by mountain ranges running roughly parallel, north to south. The landscape plays and replays a single magnificent theme of alternating broad basin and craggy range from the Wasatch Mountains of Utah to the Sierra Nevadas of California, in seemingly endless geographic rhythm. At first glance, the landscape might appear monotonous – nothing but sagebrush, a vast sea of pale green shrubs. But appearances are deceptive. As in the ocean, there is much life not immediately apparent. And above the valleys, rising thousands of feet from the sagebrush sea, mountain ranges form a sort of high-elevation archipelago, islands of cooler air and more abundant water. Here there is a rich variety of plants and animals that could not survive in the lower desert.

Great Basin National Park includes much of the South Snake Range, a superb example of a desert mountain island. From the sagebrush at its alluvial base to the 13,063-foot summit of Wheeler Peak, the park includes streams and lakes; alpine plants; abundant wildlife, from mountain lions and bobcats to pronghorn antelope and mule deer; a variety of forest types, including groves of ancient bristlecone pines; and numerous limestone caverns, including beautiful Lehman Caves.

Lehman Caves (a single cavern,

Bristlecone pines that are several thousand years old grow slowly in the clean but harsh desert-mountain environment. (RALPH BRUNNER)

despite the name) extends a quarter mile into the limestone and low-grade marble that flank the base of the Snake Range. One of the most richly decorated caverns, Lehman Caves displays an array of cave formations, or as scientists call them, "speleothems," such as stalactites, stalagmites, columns, draperies, and flowstone. Lehman Caves is most famous for the rare and mysterious structures called "shields." Shields consist of two roughly circular halves, almost like flattened clam shells. How they are formed remains a subject of controversy.

Park rangers lead tours of Lehman Caves and nature walks. Hiking opportunities abound, including a strenuous climb up Wheeler Peak. Close beneath its summit, a bit of the Ice Age exists in the form of a small glacier, the only one of its kind in the Great Basin. It calls to mind the glaciers that capped the Snake Range only a few thousand years ago.

Wheeler Peak Scenic Drive provides good views. The 12-mile-long route climbs 3,400 feet, passing through a variety of habitats: from pinyon–juniper woodlands, along a creekbed lined with aspen trees, through a zone of shrubby mountain mahogany and manzanita, into deep forests of Englemann spruce and Douglas fir, to the flower-spangled meadows and subalpine forest of limber pine, spruce, and aspen at the Wheeler Park campground.

**GREAT BASIN
NATIONAL PARK
Established 1986
77,109 acres
Baker, NV 89311
(702) 234-7331**

Numerous rock-art sites in the park reveal that prehistoric peoples lived in this area on the shores of ancient Lake Bonneville. Later Native Americans resided in villages near the present towns of Baker and Garrison from about A.D. 1100 to 1300. Known as members of the Fremont culture, they irrigated corn, beans, and squash in the valley and hunted in the mountains.

Shoshone and Paiute peoples lived in the area from about 1300 until recently, in small kin groups near springs and other water sources. They gathered and hunted a variety of wild foods, but their dietary mainstay, especially important in winter, was the pinyon nut. Descendants of these people still live in the area and share this harvest with other residents: pinyon jays, rock squirrels, wood rats, and other small animals.

The Snake Range provides a good example of biogeography, the relationship between living things and the landscape. As the elevation increases, the climate changes, creating habitats for different plants and animals. During the last Ice Age, glaciers sprawled across the high peaks. The air was cooler, allowing forests of bristlecone and limber pine to grow on the valley bottom, along the shores of long sinuous lakes. The largest body of water was Lake Bonneville, of which the Great Salt Lake is today a shrunken remnant. About 15,000 years ago, its waves lapped a beach just 10 miles from the current park boundary.

That changed around 10,000 years ago, when the climate turned warmer. Glaciers melted, lakes dried up, and the desert plants seen today invaded the desiccated valleys. The Snake Range became an island surrounded by desert, a refuge for temperate-climate dwellers.

In the South Snake Range, thirteen peaks rise above 11,000 feet. On those lofty exposed summits, winter is never far off. Snow can fall during any month, even in July. At night, freezing temperatures are common. To survive, plants must cope with a short growing season, poor soil, thin air, and intense solar radiation. High winds also buffet the peaks, punishing anything that rises above the horizon – including hikers. Whatever lives here must keep a low profile. Lichens cling to rocks like paint. Dwarfed plants grow tight to the ground, firmly anchored in crevices. Shrubs appear pruned by a careful bonsai gardener. Trees exist in small cavities or hollows.

The trees found highest in the Snake Range, limber and bristle-cone pines, appear between 9,500 and 11,000 feet. On rocky slopes near the end of the Wheeler Peak Scenic Drive, trees have endured for thousands of years. A bristle-cone pine found here was determined to be the world's oldest living thing, at 4,950 years of age.

Great Smoky Mountains National Park

A view across cloud tops from the summit of Clingmans Dome.

The Great Smoky Mountains, the majestic zenith of the Appalachian Highlands, are a wildlands sanctuary preserving the world's finest examples of temperate deciduous forest. The name "Smoky" comes from the smoke-like haze enveloping the mountains, which stretch in sweeping troughs and mighty billows to the horizon.

Straddling the border of Tennessee and North Carolina, the Smokies form the loftiest range east of the Black Hills, and one of the oldest uplands on Earth. Centrally located, within two days' drive for half of the nation's population, Great Smoky Mountains National Park has the most visitors of all the national parks in the United States – between 8 and 10 million visitors come to the park annually.

The park – which features more species of trees than northern Europe – boasts unspoiled forests similar to those early pioneers found. Restored log cabins and barns stand as reminders of those who carved a living from this wilderness. Fertile soils and abundant rain have encouraged the development of a world-renowned variety of flora, including more than 1,500 kinds of flowering plants. In the coves, broadleaf trees predominate. Along the crest – at more than 6,000 feet elevation – are conifer forests like those of central Canada.

The biological diversity found from mountain foot to peak in Great Smoky Mountains National Park is comparable to that encountered on the 2,000-mile hike on the Appalachian Trail from Georgia to Maine. The Smokies provide the only habitat in the world for several plant and animal species, including Cain's reedbent grass, Rugel's ragwort, and Jordan's (red-cheeked) salamander. The park is also one of the few places remaining in the eastern United States where black bears can live in wild, natural surroundings. Some 400 to 600 bears roam the park today. At

one time, the black bear's range included most of North America except the extreme west coast. Because of the loss of habitat, the black bear is now confined to wooded areas or dense brushland.

GREAT SMOKY MOUNTAINS NATIONAL PARK
Established 1934
520,269 acres
Gatlinburg, TN 37738
(Also in North Carolina)
(615) 436-1200

Wildflowers and migrating birds abound in late April and early May. During June and July, rhododendrons bloom in spectacular profusion. Autumn's pageantry of color usually peaks in mid-October. For many, this is the finest time of year, with cool, clear days ideal for hiking. In winter, an unpredictable season, a peace pervades the park. Fog rolling over

the mountains may blanket the conifers in frost.

A scenic, high mountain road winds up through Newfound Gap, with a spur out to Clingmans Dome and its observation tower. Along the road are superb views, and those from the tower are truly panoramic. But roads offer only an introduction to the Smokies. Some 800 miles of trails thread the whole of the Smokies' natural fabric – and its waterfalls, coves, balds, and rushing streams. The trails cover every degree of difficulty, from paved walking paths to steep mountain trails.

Visitors can explore the mountainous terrain that was once home to Cherokee Indians, who moved here roughly 1,000 years ago. Around 1800, permanent European settlements were established, depending primarily on farming. Life for many families changed with the coming of commercial logging operations around 1900 that stripped trees from two-

thirds of what is now park land.

The Smokies became a national park only after a long, difficult struggle. Establishing such older parks as Yellowstone was fairly easy. Congress merely carved them out of lands already owned by the government – often places where no one wanted to live anyway. Not so with the Smokies. They were owned by hundreds of small farmers and a handful of large timber and paper companies who did not want to abandon their property. The push to establish a national park began in the late 1890s, but it was not until 1926 that the park was authorized, and later, in 1934, that it was fully established. The park was created from more than 6,000 tracts of private and commercial land that were bought with money raised by public and private donations. Today the park is designated as an International Biosphere Reserve to preserve the land's genetic diversity.

The Great Smokies, along the Little River (left) and near Laurel Falls (above), contain some of the largest remaining tracts of temperate deciduous forest in the world.

Spring foliage below Newfound Gap, looking down the valley of the West Prong of the Little Pigeon River.

Guadalupe Mountains National Park

A dense forest of ponderosa pine, southwestern white pine, Douglas fir, and aspen grows in the high country of the Guadalupes. (NATIONAL PARK SERVICE)

Guadalupe Mountains National Park preserves the rugged spirit and remote wilderness of the American West – from the flowering cacti of the Chihuahuan Desert to the 8,749-foot Guadalupe Peak, the highest point in the Lone Star State.

The Guadalupe Mountains are part of one of the finest examples of an ancient marine fossil reef on Earth. During the Permian period, approximately 280 to 230 million years ago, a vast tropical ocean covered portions of Texas and New Mexico. Over millions of years, calcareous sponges and algae combined with other lime-secreting marine organisms, and vast quantities of lime from the seawater formed the 400-mile-long, horse-shoe-shaped Capitan Reef. Eventually the sea evaporated, the reef subsided, and a thick blanket of sediments and mineral salts buried the reef. The reef was entombed for millions of years until a mountain-building uplift exposed a part of the fossil reef in the Guadalupe Mountains. Other parts of the reef are exposed in two other mountain ranges – the Apache Mountains and the Glass Mountains.

In the mountain high country of the Guadalupes thrives a dense forest of ponderosa pine, southwestern white pine, Douglas fir, and aspen. This predominantly coniferous forest is a relict of ancient times – about 15,000 years ago – when the prevailing climate throughout Texas was cooler and moister. As the climate warmed, fragments of this forest survived in the higher elevations of some southern mountains such as the Guadalupes. The forest is especially lush in The Bowl, a 2-mile wide depression atop the Guadalupe Mountains. Throughout this highland wilderness roam elk, mule deer, raccoons, wild turkeys, vultures, mountain lions, and black bears.

The many deep, sheer-sided canyons of the Guadalupe Mountains display an impressive diversity of plants and animals, most notably in McKittrick Canyon. Lying between the desert below and the highlands above, McKittrick, like other canyons, has a mix of life that is part desert, part canyon woodland, and part highland forest. Prickly pear cacti, agaves, willows, ferns, Texas madrones, Texas walnuts, alligator junipers, and ponderosa pines grow in the canyon. Wildlife includes jackrabbits, coyotes, porcupines, gray foxes, mule deer, mountain lions, and elk.

Moderate temperatures and protection from the sun and wind provided by the high cliff walls nurture this canyon community. McKittrick Canyon also has a feature no other canyon in the park has – a perennial spring-fed stream. Gray oak, velvet ash, big-tooth maple, and other shade trees border the clear creek, and mule deer drink from its pools. In late October and early November, the trees' foliage turns brilliant reds, yellows, and oranges, creating a scene reminiscent of more northern woods. McKittrick Canyon exudes a lushness that is rarely found in this part of Texas.

At the foot of the Guadalupe Mountains lie the sparsely populated plains of the Chihuahuan Desert. Only a small portion of this desert is actually preserved within the park, but this vast arid realm dominates views from the mountains. The Chihuahuan Desert receives between 10 and 20 inches of rain a year; in the summer, temperatures rise to 90°F and above. Although it can look barren at first glance, the desert is full of life. Many of the Chihuahuan Desert's most common plants and animals are found in the park. Agaves, prickly pear cacti, walking-stick chollas, yuccas, and sotol are abundant, and lizards, snakes, kangaroo rats, coyotes, and mule deer are seen frequently.

The remote highlands of this mountainous terrain were the exclusive domain of the Mescalero Apaches until the mid-1800s. Later came explorers and pioneers, who welcomed the imposing sight of the Guadalupe peaks rising boldly out of the Texas desert, not only as an important landmark but also for the water and shelter the mountains provided. But cultures conflicted, and the Apaches did not welcome the intrusion of new people into their domain. In 1849 the U.S. Army began a campaign against them that was to last three decades. The Guadalupes became the Apaches' only sanctuary from the soldiers and a staging ground for their own attacks. By 1880 the last of the Apaches had been driven out of the Guadalupes.

Amid this conflict, Butterfield stagecoaches began carrying mail through the Guadalupes on the nation's first transcontinental mail route. The present-day ruins of The Pinery stagecoach station are a reminder of this historic service.

In the years that followed, some ranching operations developed. One ranch, in McKittrick Canyon,

GUADALUPE MOUNTAINS NATIONAL PARK
Established 1972
86,416 acres
H.C. 60, Box 400
Salt Flat, TX 79847
(915) 828-3251

was built in the 1930s by Wallace Pratt, a brilliant petroleum geologist who was charmed by the rugged beauty of the Guadalupes. In 1959, Pratt donated his land to the National Park Service so it could be preserved and enjoyed by others. Additional land was later purchased from J.C. Hunter, and in 1972 Guadalupe Mountains National Park was created by an act of Congress.

Haleakala National Park

Legend has it that Haleakala, or "House of the Sun," is where the demigod Maui captured the sun to ensure its people more daylight. This sun-drenched tropical park on the island of Maui preserves the Haleakala Crater, a dormant volcano, the unique and fragile ecosystems of Kipahulu Valley, the scenic pools along ʻOheʻo Gulch, and many rare and endangered species.

Haleakala Crater is now a cool, cone-studded reminder of a once-active volcano. Streaks of red, yellow, gray, and black trace the courses of recent and ancient lava, ash, and cinder flows. The volcanic rocks slowly break down as natural forces reduce them to minute particles that are swept away by wind, heavy rain, and intermittent streams.

Maui, one of the younger of the chain of Hawaiian islands, began as two separate volcanoes. Over time, the volcanoes erupted periodically, and lava, wind-blown ash, and alluvium eventually joined the two by an isthmus or valley, forming Maui, "The Valley Isle."

Haleakala, the larger eastern volcano, eventually reached its greatest height, at 12,000 feet above sea level, and some 30,000 feet from its base on the ocean floor. The 19-square-mile, 2,720-foot-deep crater was formed by streams eroding the mountain and eventually joining two valleys.

In contrast to the red and yellow, gray and black lava ash and cinder cones of Haleakala Crater are the lush greenness and abundant waters of the Kipahulu section of the park. A chain of sparkling pools, connected by a waterfall or short cascade, is usually placid. But ʻOheʻo Stream, which joins the pools, can become a thundering white-water torrent obscuring these quiet pools as it churns and plunges headlong toward the ocean. The upper rain forest above the pools receives up to 250 inches of rainfall a year, and

The rare and unique silversword grow in Haleakala Crater. (RON WATTS/FIRST LIGHT)

flash floods do occur here.

A pastoral scene of rolling grasslands and forested valleys surrounds the pools. Ginger and ti form an understory in forests of kukui, mango, guava, and bamboo, while beach naupaka, false kamani, and pandanus abound along the rugged coastal cliffs. Pictographs, painted by long-forgotten artists, and farm plots once flourishing with cultivated taro and sweet potatoes, remind us of an age when the *ali'i* – Hawaiian chiefs – ruled this land.

In the higher elevations, a vast native *koa* and *'ohi'a* rain forest thrives, just as it has for thousands of years, still relatively undisturbed by the influences of man. It is here that the endangered Maui *nukupu'u*, Maui parrotbill, and other native birds still survive in a delicately balanced environment.

Time and extreme isolation were essential for the development of Hawaii's unique native plant-

and birdlife. Many species of birds are found nowhere else. The golden plover, commonly seen from September to May, is famous for its migratory flights to and from Alaska. The *'apapane, 'i'iwi, 'amakihi,* and *nene* are among those birds native only to the Hawaiian

> **HALEAKALA NATIONAL PARK**
> **Authorized 1916**
> **28,099 acres**
> **P.O. Box 369**
> **Makawao, HI 96768**
> **(808) 572-9306**

Islands. The *'i'iwi* is one of the most beautiful of all Hawaiian birds, with a bright scarlet body, black wings and tail, and inch-long curved bill. The *'apapane* is also scarlet, but has a white belly and black legs and bill. The bright green and yellow *'amakihi* is known for the speed at which it

searches for nectar and insects. However, most of the birds seen along park roads – pheasants, chukars, skylarks, mockingbirds – are introduced forms. These birds have taken their toll of native birdlife – as the carriers of bird diseases and competitors for territory and food.

The most distinctive plant of Haleakala is the silversword, called *ahinahina,* or "gray-gray," by the Hawaiians. After growing for five to twenty years, this spectacular plant, with its many dagger-like silvery leaves, develops a cluster of 100 to 500 yellow and reddish purple flower heads. Each flower produces hundreds of seeds, and as the seeds develop, the remainder of the plant slowly dies. Strangely enough, the silversword dies after blooming only once.

In contrast to Hawaii's unique birdlife, all mammals – except for a small brown bat and monk seal – arrived on these islands with

man's intentional or accidental aid, and their presence has greatly upset the natural balance here. Wild pigs, initially brought by early Hawaiians, root today through the west areas of the park. Goats, introduced by Europeans, browse throughout the crater. These two exotics are the most serious threat to the native plant and animal populations. Other introduced species inhabit the park, such as the predatory mongoose, released in sugar cane fields to control rats and mice, which were also introduced to the islands. These animals continue to threaten the natural relationship that would have evolved between organisms and their environment in the absence of interference by modern man. Thus, the Park Service has embarked on an exotic plant- and animal-control program to preserve the ecosystem of Haleakala National Park.

Hawaii Volcanoes National Park

Volcanoes are monuments to Earth's origin and evidence that its primordial forces are still at work. During a volcanic eruption, we are reminded that our planet is an ever-changing environment whose basic processes are beyond human control. As much as we have altered the face of the Earth to suit our needs, we can only stand in awe before the power of an eruption.

Volcanoes are also prodigious land-builders – they have created the Hawaiian Island chain. Kilauea and Mauna Loa, two of the world's most active volcanoes, are still adding land to the island of Hawaii. Mauna Loa is the most massive mountain on Earth, occupying an area of 10,000 cubic miles. Measured from its base on the sea floor, it rises 30,000 feet, more than 1,000 feet higher than Mount Everest. In contrast to the explosive continental volcanoes,

A tremendous column of steam rises where molten lava meets the ocean.
(RON WATTS/FIRST LIGHT)

the more fluid and less gaseous eruptions of Kilauea and Mauna Loa produce fiery fountains and rivers of molten lava. These flows, added layer upon layer, produced a barren volcanic landscape that served as a foundation for life. Hundreds of species of plants and animals found their way across the vast Pacific on wind, water, and the wings of birds. A few survived, adapted, and prospered during this time of isolation. Today, over 90 percent of Hawaii's native flora and fauna are endemic – found nowhere else on Earth.

The arrival of humans – first Polynesians, then Europeans – and the plants and animals they brought with them drastically altered the conditions that fostered the original diversity of life in the Hawaiian Archipelago. Forests disappeared as people cleared the land to plant crops and establish communities. Polynesian and other settlers introduced numerous alien plants and animals, some of which thrived in their new home and multiplied. Their impact has been catastrophic: Pigs destroy the understory of tree-fern and 'ohi'a forests. Their muddy wallows provide breeding grounds for mosquitoes that transmit avian malaria and pox to native birds. Mongooses, cats, and rats eat native birds and their eggs. Alien plants such as firetree and banana poka displace vast areas of Hawaiian forests. The onslaught of introduced plants and animals caused the extinction of countless native species and continues to threaten Hawaii's unique life forms.

Created to preserve the natural setting of Kilauea and Mauna Loa, Hawaii Volcanoes National Park is also a refuge for the island's native plants and animals and a link to its human past. The park has also been designated as an International Biosphere Reserve and a World Heritage Site. Today, Hawaii Volcanoes displays the results of 70 million years of volcanism, migration, and evolution – processes that thrust a bare land from the sea and clothed it with complex and unique ecosystems

and a distinct human culture.

Superb voyagers, Polynesians from the Marquesas Islands migrated to Hawaii over 1,600 years ago. Navigating by the sun and stars, reading the winds, currents, and the flight of seabirds, they sailed across 2,400 miles of open ocean in great double-hulled canoes. They brought along items essential to their survival: *pua'a* (pigs), *'ilio* (dogs), and *moa* (chickens); the roots of *kalo* (taro) and *'uala* (sweet potato); and the seeds and saplings of *niu* (coconut), *mai'a* (banana), *ko* (sugar cane), and other edible and medicinal plants. They were well established on the islands when, about 800 years ago, Polynesians from the Society Islands arrived in Hawaii. Claiming descent from the greatest gods, they became the new rulers of Hawaii. After a time of voyaging back and forth, contact with southern Polynesia ceased. During the 400 years of isolation that followed, a unique Hawaiian culture developed.

Hawaii was a highly stratified society with strictly maintained

castes. The *ali'i* (chiefs) headed the social pyramid and ruled over the land. Highly regarded and sometimes feared, the *Kahuna* (professionals) were experts on religious ritual or specialists in canoe building, herbal medicine, or healing. The *maka'ainana* (commoners) farmed and fished; built walls, houses, and fishponds; and paid taxes to the king and his chiefs. *Kauwa*, the lowest class, were outcasts or slaves.

**HAWAII VOLCANOES
NATIONAL PARK
Established 1916
229,177 acres
Hawaii National Park, HI 96718
(808) 967-7311**

A system of laws known as *kanawai* enforced the social order. Certain people, places, things, and times were sacred – they were *kapu*, or forbidden. Women ate apart from men and were not allowed to eat pork, coconuts, bananas, or a variety of other

foods. *Kapu* regulated fishing, planting, and the harvesting of other resources, thus ensuring their conservation. Any breaking of *kapu* disturbed the stability of society; the punishment often was death.

Village life was rich and varied; Hawaiians fished in coastal waters and collected shellfish, seaweed, and salt along the shore. They raised pigs, dogs, and chickens, and harvested sweet potatoes, taro, and other crops. Men pounded taro into poi, while women beat the inner bark of *wauke* (paper mulberry) into kapa for clothes and bedding. They worshipped *akua* (gods) and *'aumakua* (guardian spirits) and chronicled their history through *oli* (chant), *mele* (song), and *hula* (dance). Over several hundred years the people of Hawaii cultivated traditions that they passed on through generations. But the sounds of taro pounding and kapa beating, rhythmical signatures of Hawaiian village life, would fade away after Captain James Cook arrived in 1778 and introduced the rest of the world to Hawaii.

Hot Springs National Park

Water. That's what attracts people to Hot Springs National Park in Arkansas. In fact, they have been coming here since the first person stumbled across these hot springs perhaps 10,000 years ago. Stone artifacts found in the park provide evidence that Indians knew about and used the hot springs. For them the area was a neutral ground where different tribes came to hunt, trade, and bathe in peace. Surely they drank the spring waters too, for they found the water, with its minerals and gases, to have a pleasant taste and smell. These traces of minerals, combined with a temperature of 143°F, are credited with giving the waters whatever therapeutic properties they may have. The thermal waters are naturally sterile, which is why the National Aeronautics and Space Administration chose the Hot Springs, among other waters, as a holding medium for moon rocks while the search went on for signs of life. The absence of bacteria in the water helped prevent the

Fordyce Bathhouse is one of the many attractions of Hot Springs, once promoted as "The Nation's Health Sanitarium." (NATIONAL PARK SERVICE)

spread of disease during the early years that the springs were uncovered. Today most of the springs have been covered to prevent contamination.

Waters from the cold springs, which have different chemical components and properties, are also used for drinking. Scientists have determined that the waters gushing from hot springs are more than 4,000 years old. And the waters gush at an average of 850,000 gallons a day.

The words "hot springs" often conjure up images of volcanoes, geysers, and underground chambers of molten rock or magma – features usually associated with hot springs. But in this area, the Earth is relatively quiet. There is no evidence of magma lying close below the Earth's surface to heat underground water. Instead, geologists believe that just the right combination of rock types and old faults exists to permit water to percolate deep, where it is heated by surrounding rock. Two types of rock in the area, Bigfork chert and Arkansas novaculite, act like giant sponges – they are porous or highly fractured. Lying in tilted layers, these rocks have absorbed the rain and conducted it slowly downward for nearly 4,000 years to depths between 2,000 and 8,000 feet. As the water percolates down, the increasingly warmer rock heats it and filters out the impurities. In the process, the water dissolves minerals in the rocks. Eventually the water meets the faults and joints in the Hot Springs sandstone leading up to the lower west side of Hot Springs Mountain, where it flows to the surface. The water retains most of its heat during its upward journey

– which takes about a year – and arrives at the surface at an average temperature of 143°F.

Hot Springs, a highly developed

> **HOT SPRINGS**
> **NATIONAL PARK**
> **Established 1921**
> **5,839 acres**
> **P.O. Box 1860**
> **Hot Springs, AR 71902**
> **(501) 624-3383**

park, lies in a small city surrounded by low-lying mountains abounding in plantlife and wildlife. The parks lies about 55 miles southwest of Little Rock in the Zig Zag Mountains, on the eastern edge of the Ouachita Range. The Hot Springs are on the lower western side of Hot Springs Mountain. Dense forests of oak, hickory, and short-leaf pine dominate this region. Flowering trees are also common, and successive seasons have displays of colored leaves and abundant flowers. Redbud and dogwood bloom in the early spring, gracing the understory of the pine and hardwood woodlands. Flowering southern magnolias lend historic Bathhouse Row in downtown Hot Springs a special beauty, particularly in early summer. Songbirds and small animals are abundant in the forest. Hot Springs has a favorable climate all year. The winters are mild, and except for infrequent intervals, outdoor recreation can be enjoyed year-round.

Hot Springs is one of the oldest areas in the national park system. Tradition has it that the first Europeans to see the springs were the Spanish explorer Hernando de Soto and his troops in 1541. French trappers, hunters, and traders became familiar with the area in the late seventeenth century. In 1803, the United States acquired the area when it purchased the Louisiana Territory from France, and the very next year President Thomas Jefferson dispatched an expedition led by William Dunbar and George Hunter to explore the newly acquired springs. Their report to the president was widely publicized and stirred up interest in the "Hot Springs of the Washita." In the years that followed, more and more people came here to soak in the waters. Soon the idea of "reserving" the springs for the nation took root, and a proposal was submitted to Congress by the territorial representative, Ambrose H. Sevier. Then, in 1832, the federal government took the unprecedented step of setting aside four sections of land here, the first U.S. reservation made simply to protect a natural resource. Little effort was made to mark the boundaries adequately, and by the mid-1800s, claims and counterclaims on the springs and the land surrounding them were being filed.

Isle Royale National Park

In Lake Superior's northwest corner sits a wilderness archipelago, a roadless land of wolves, moose, and other wild creatures, unspoiled forests, refreshing lakes, and rugged, scenic shores – accessible only by boat or floatplane. There are more than 164 miles of foot trails on Isle Royale, the largest island in the largest freshwater lake in the world.

The island has a striking striated layout of elongated forested-rock and lake patterns that parallel its backbone, the Greenstone Ridge. The island's landscape – a product of natural sculpting – seems to have been forcibly combed from northeast to southwest. Ten thousand years ago the island appeared beneath glacial ice, rising as the lake level dropped. The island developed soil and was colonized by plants and animals. Its many inland lakes first formed in basins gouged out by glaciers.

Long before Europeans saw Isle Royale, Indians mined copper here. The Indians came to the island only in mild seasons, taking what resources they could, and leaving before winter. As early as 2000 B.C., the Indians mined here, continuing for more than 1,000 years, and Isle Royale and Superior area copper made its way by trade as far as New York, Illinois, and Indiana. Indians were probably most active here from 800 to 1600. By the 1840s, the only Indian encampments European miners encountered were a maple-sugaring camp on Sugar Mountain and a seasonal fishing camp on Grace Island.

Commercial fishing has historically been one of the mainstay economic activities on the island. It began before 1800, to feed the fur traders. Since about 1840, it has been a largely individual enterprise. The major economic species were lake trout, whitefish, and herring lurking in the range of water depths and bottoms along miles of Isle Royale shoreline. Most of the commercial fishing enterprises had closed by mid-century; that world is now preserved by the historic

A moose takes a dip in one of several refreshing lakes within Isle Royale. (NATIONAL PARK SERVICE)

Edisen Fishery and programs conducted by the National Park Service. Sport fishing has now been replaced by commercial fishing. Species sought are lake, brook, and rainbow trout; northern pike; walleye; and the yellow perch. Spring and fall produce the biggest catches, but fishing is considered good throughout the season.

Isle Royale is known for its wolves and moose, which in the recent past have come in search of better hunting and browsing grounds. Other animals you might expect here are missing, however, although Isle Royale is but 15 miles to the Canadian shores where they are found. But even what is missing, like the black bear and white-tailed deer, somehow enriches the sense of Isle Royale's wild solitude.

ISLE ROYALE NATIONAL PARK
Authorized 1931
571,790 acres
800 East Lakeshore Drive
Houghton, MI 49931
(906) 482-0984

Had we visited Isle Royale at the turn of this century, we would have found it quite different. We would have seen no wolves or moose. Instead, we might have seen a herd of caribou or glimpsed a lynx, no longer seen today. The forest undergrowth would have been thick with American yew rather than thimbleberry. Since the turn of the century, the coyote has come and gone. The white-tailed deer was introduced and has since disappeared. Sometime early in this century, moose immigrated to the island, probably swimming from Canada's mainland. With abundant food and no predators, the unmolested moose population grew. By the early 1930s, the moose had destroyed their food supply and began to die off in great numbers. A fire in 1936 burned browse over a quarter of the island, and by 1937 the moose population crashed. But the fire stimulated growth of new browse, and the unchecked moose population began to grow, only to crash again when the food ran out. During the cold winter of 1948–49, an ice bridge formed between Canada and the island, and a small pack of eastern timber wolves crossed to Isle Royale. Since then, additional packs have become established here as offshoots of the original pack. Individual wolves have ranged in number from twelve to fifty. The population is now at the low end of that range.

The wolves are important in maintaining a healthy moose population. The very young, the very old, and those moose prone to predation because of illness or injury are the most likely prey. By culling the weak and old, wolves contribute to the health of the moose population. When predators decrease, the number of prey increases and the dynamic cycle begins again.

As a wilderness, Isle Royale is more than just a sanctuary for wolves and moose. The island's uniqueness lies in its complex yet simple system of natural processes, a system in which moose are dependent upon both wolves and beaver – wolves to control their numbers, and beaver to provide dams and, in turn, the aquatic vegetation upon which moose feed. The beaver also serve as a summer food for the wolf, and the beaver ponds eventually become meadows that support a variety of smaller animals. The red fox eats the hare who, if left unchecked, would destroy the forest that supports the moose that supports the wolf. In such a system a dynamic equilibrium is struck in which each species has an important role. Isle Royale has been designated an International Biosphere Reserve under the Man and the Biosphere program.

Joshua Tree National Park

Cholla cactus and wildflowers amid a land of sculptured rocks. (RALPH BRUNNER)

The desert is immense and infinitely variable, yet delicately fragile. It is a land shaped by sudden torrents of rain and climatic extremes. Rainfall is sparse and unpredictable. Streambeds are usually dry, and waterholes are few. This land may appear defeated and dead, but within its parched environment are intricate living systems, each fragment performing a slightly different function, and each depending upon the whole system for survival.

Two large desert ecosystems come together at Joshua Tree National Park, which lies 140 miles east of Los Angeles. Few areas more vividly illustrate the contrast between high and low desert. Below 3,000 feet, the Colorado Desert, occupying the eastern half of the park, is dominated by the abundant creosote bush. Adding interest to this arid land are small stands of spidery ocotillo and jumping cholla cactus. The higher, slightly cooler, and wetter Mohave Desert is the special habitat of the undisciplined Joshua tree, extensive stands of which occur throughout the western half of the park.

Standing like islands in a desolate sea, the oases, a third ecosystem, provide dramatic contrast to their arid surroundings. Five fan-palm oases dot the park, indicating those few areas where water occurs naturally at or near the surface, meeting the special life requirements of these stately trees. Oases once serving earlier desert visitors now abound in wildlife.

The life force is patient here. Desert vegetation, oftentimes appearing to have succumbed to a sometimes harsh and unforgiving environment, lies dormant, anxiously awaiting the rainfall and moderate weather that will trigger its growth, painting the park a profusion of colors. At the edges of daylight and under clear night stars is a fascinating multitude of generally unfamiliar desert wildlife. Waiting out daytime heat, these creatures run, hop, crawl, and burrow in the slow rhythm of desert life. Under bright sun and blue sky, bighorn sheep and golden eagles add an air of unconcerned majesty to this land.

The lifeblood of the desert ecosystem is the sun's energy, converted to a living form by green plants. Unlike most ecosystems, in which plants compete for space in the sun, the desert's sparsity is created in part by too much solar energy. Plants use one of two life strategies to survive. Annuals avoid the extremes, compress their life cycle, and exist while the environment is favorable. Sudden carpets of spring wildflowers are displays of awakened dormancy as seeds, like time travelers, revive to sprout, flower, and renew their kind. The alternative strategy is that of the patient perennial. Conservative year-round residents like the Joshua tree flourish during the moist periods and bide their time during long droughts.

Many animals derive their energy from plants, but desert plants give up the fruits of their

production only reluctantly. Sharp spines and chemical-laden leaves complicate the lives of plant-eaters. The kangaroo rat avoids these obstacles by eating seeds. While safe to eat, seeds can be hard to find. Many are small, looking surprisingly like the sand grains that offer them sanctuary. The kangaroo rat uses sensitive

JOSHUA TREE NATIONAL PARK
Established 1994
794,000 acres
74485 National Monument Drive
Twentynine Palms, CA 92277
(619) 367-7511

front paws to sift through sand, discovering seeds by smell as well as touch. Seeds consumed by the kangaroo rat are converted into animal tissue. Energy continues to flow through the chain as kangaroo rats and other plant-eaters, such as jackrabbits, fall prey to meat-eaters. It takes many rabbits and rodents to feed a single owl, coyote, bobcat, or eagle, so there must be far more prey than predators. The original solar energy

converted to plant tissue has now been transformed several times as it moves through the food chain.

As the original source of living energy, plants fulfill a vital role in the food chain. A large productive plant such as the Joshua tree represents a focal point for a complex community of wildlife. Some birds nest in the living Joshua. Others feed on insects infesting the tree. Discarded limbs or the toppled body of the Joshua provides homes for the yucca night lizard and termites. Even in death, the plant energy of the Joshua is converted by termites to animal energy. The chain is fragile, no stronger than its weakest link, yet it endures.

The park encompasses some of the most interesting geologic displays found in California's deserts. Rugged mountains of twisted rock and exposed granite monoliths testify to the tremendous Earth forces that shaped and formed this land. Arroyos, playas, alluvial fans, bajadas, pediments, desert varnish, granites, aplite, and gneiss interact to form a giant desert mosaic of immense beauty and complexity.

As old as the desert may look, it is but a temporary phenomenon in

the incomprehensible time-scale of geology. In more verdant times, one of the Southwest's earliest inhabitants, Pinto Man, lived here, hunting and gathering along a slow-moving river that ran through the now dry Pinto Basin. Later, Indians traveled through this area in tune with harvests of pinyon nuts, mesquite beans, acorns, and cactus fruit, leaving behind rock paintings and pottery ollas as reminders of their passing. In the late 1800s explorers, cattlemen, and miners came to the desert. They built dams to create water tanks and dug up and tunneled the earth in search of gold. They are gone now, and left behind are their remnants, the Lost Horse and Desert Queen mines and the Desert Queen Ranch. In the 1930s homesteaders came seeking free land and the chance to start new lives. Proclaimed a national monument in 1936, this desert landscape was designated a Biosphere Reserve in 1984, and upgraded to a national park in 1994. Today many people come to the park seeking clear skies and clean air and the quietude and beauty only deserts offer.

Katmai National Park and Preserve

A grizzly bear with a freshly caught salmon. (RALPH BRUNNER)

The cataclysmic 1912 eruption of Novarupta Volcano put Katmai, a largely unknown landscape on the southern shore of the Alaska Peninsula, on the map. Katmai was declared a national monument in 1918 to preserve this volcanic laboratory; boasting fifteen active volcanoes along the Shelikof Strait, Katmai is one of the world's most active volcanic centers today. Since then the preservation of the brown bear has become an equally compelling charge for Katmai. To protect this magnificent animal and its varied habitat, Katmai's boundaries were extended over the years, and in 1980 the area was designated a national park and preserve.

Katmai is so vast that the bulk of it must elude all but a few persistent visitors. To boat its enormous lakes and their island-studded bays, to float its rushing waterways, to hike the wind-whipped passes of its imposing mountains, or to explore its Shelikof Strait coastline requires great effort and logistical planning.

Katmai's awe-inspiring natural powers confront us most visibly in its volcanics and its brown bears.

The June 1912 eruption of Novarupta Volcano altered the Katmai area dramatically. Ten times more forceful than the 1980 eruption of Mount St. Helens, it caused enormous quantities of hot, glowing pumice from Novarupta and nearby fissures to destroy all life in its path. For several days a haze of ash darkened the sky over most of the Northern Hemisphere.

When it was over, more than 40 square miles of lush green land lay buried beneath volcanic deposits measuring as much as 700 feet in depth. At nearby Kodiak, for two days a person holding a lantern at arm's length could not see the light from it. Acid rain caused clothes to disintegrate on clotheslines in distant Vancouver, Canada. Eventually, Novarupta became dormant.

It was an apparently unnamed valley when the twentieth century's most dramatic volcanic episode took place. Botanist Robert Griggs, exploring the volcano's aftermath for the National Geographic Society in 1916, stared

awestruck off Katmai Pass across the valley's roaring landscape riddled with thousands of steam vents – "The Valley of Ten Thousand Smokes," Griggs named it.

"The whole valley as far as the

> **KATMAI NATIONAL PARK AND PRESERVE**
> Established 1980
> National park: 3,716,000 acres
> National preserve: 374,000 acres
> P.O. Box 7
> King Salmon, AK 99613
> (907) 246-3305

eye could reach was full of hundreds, no thousands – literally, tens of thousands – of smokes curling up from its fissured floor," Griggs would write. The steam vents, or fumaroles, steamed 500 to 1,000 feet in the air.

Today, visitors can take the trip from Brooks Camp out to the Valley of Ten Thousand Smokes, where the turbulent Ukak River and its tributaries cut deep gorges in the accumulated ash.

In summer, North America's largest land predators gather along

salmon runs to feast, building weight from this wealth of protein and fat, preparing for the long winter ahead. Mature male bears in Katmai may weigh up to 900 pounds. Alaska's brown bears and grizzlies are now considered one species, although people commonly consider grizzlies to be those that live 100 miles and more inland, and browns are bigger than grizzlies, thanks to their rich diet of fish. Kodiak brown bears are a differing subspecies that is geographically isolated on Kodiak Island in the Gulf of Alaska.

Katmai's lake edges and marshes serve as nesting sites for tundra swans, ducks, loons, grebes, and that 20,000-mile annual commuter, the arctic tern. Seabirds abound along the coast, grouse and ptarmigan inhabit the uplands, and some forty songbird species summer here. Seacoast rock pinnacles and treetops along lakeshores provide nesting sites for bald eagles, hawks, falcons, and owls. Brown bears and moose live throughout the coastal and lake regions, the moose feeding on willows, water plants, and grasses. Other mammals include the cari-

bou, red fox, wolf, lynx, wolverine, river otter, mink, marten, weasel, porcupine, snowshoe hare, red squirrel, and beaver. Along the coast are sea lions, sea otters, and hair seals, with beluga, killer, and gray whales sometimes using the Shelikof Strait.

People have been coming to what is now called Katmai for thousands of years. Some found a good life in the heart of the park near the present-day Brooks River. Others made their existence along the islands and shores of the rugged Shelikof Strait. Streams filled with salmon, tundra plains covered with migrating caribou, and ocean shores teeming with abundant life were the attraction.

For more than 6,000 years people have called Katmai home. The prehistoric resources left from earlier days are included in three archaeological districts listed on the National Register of Historic Places: the Savonoski River, Takli Island, and the Brooks River districts. The archaeology of Katmai National Park has contributed significantly to an understanding of prehistoric cultural developments in southwestern Alaska.

Kenai Fjords National Park

The Kenai Fjords are coastal mountain fjords whose placid seascapes reflect scenic icebound landscapes and whose salt spray mixes with mountain mist. Located on the southeastern Kenai Peninsula, the national park is a pristine and rugged land supporting many unaltered natural environments and ecosystems. The land boasts an icefield wilderness, unnamed waterfalls in unnamed canyons, glaciers that sweep down narrow mountain valleys, and a coastline along which thousands of seabirds and marine mammals raise their young each year.

Kenai Fjords National Park derives its name from the long, steep-sided, glacier-carved valleys that are now filled with ocean waters. The seaward ends of the Kenai Mountains are slipping into the sea, being dragged under by the collision of two tectonic plates of the Earth's crust. What were once

Icebergs calved from tidewater glaciers and stranded by the tide create beautiful sculptures in North Fjord. (DAVID MUENCH)

98

alpine valleys filled with glacier ice are now deepwater mountain-flanked fjords. The forces that caused this land to submerge are still present. In 1964, the Alaskan Good Friday earthquake dropped the shoreline another 6 feet in just one day. As the land sinks into the ocean, glacier-carved cirques are turned into half-moon bays, and mountain peaks are reduced to wave-beaten islands and stacks.

Though the island is subsiding, a mountain platform 1 mile high still forms the coast's backdrop. The mountains are mantled by the 700-square-mile Harding Icefield, the park's dominant feature. The icefield was not discovered until early this century, when a mapping team realized that several coastal glaciers belonged to the same massive system. Today's icefield – one of the four major ice caps in the United States – measures some 35 miles long by 20 miles wide. Only isolated mountain peaks interrupt its nearly flat, snowclad surface. These protruding *nunataks* – an

Eskimo word meaning "lonely peaks" – rise dramatically from the frozen clutches of the Ice Age.

The mountains intercept moisture-laden clouds, which replenish the icefield with 35 to 65 feet of snow annually. Time, gravity, and the weight of overlying snow transform the snow into ice, which flows out in all directions. The ice is squeezed into glaciers that creep downward like giant bulldozers, carving and gouging the landscape. Along the coast, eight glaciers reach the sea, and these tidewater glaciers calve icebergs into the fjords. The thunderous boom of calving ice can sometimes be heard some 20 miles away.

The park's wildlife is as varied as its landscape. Mountain goats, moose, bears, wolverines, marmots, and other land mammals have re-established themselves on a thin life zone between marine waters and the icefield's frozen edges. Bald eagles nest in the tops of spruce and hemlock trees. A summer burgeon-

ing of life occurs in the fjords. Steller sea lions haul out on rocky islands at the entrances of Aialik and Nuka bays. Harbor seals ride

KENAI FJORDS NATIONAL PARK
Established 1980
580,000 acres
P.O. Box 1727
Seward, AK 99664
(907) 224-3175

the icebergs. Dall's porpoises, sea otters, and gray, humpback, killer, and minke whales ply the fjord waters. Halibut, lingcod, and black bass lurk deep in these waters, through which salmon return for inland spawning runs. Thousands of seabirds, including horned and tufted puffins, black-legged kittiwakes, common murres, and the ubiquitous gulls, seasonally inhabit steep cliffs and rocky shores.

Exit Glacier, remnant of a larger glacier once extending to Resurrection Bay, is one of several

rivers of ice flowing off the icefield. Active, yet retreating, it provides the perfect setting to explore. Here are found newly exposed, scoured, and polished bedrock and a regime of plant succession from the earliest pioneer plants to a mature forest of Sitka spruce and western hemlock.

Humans have had little lasting impact on this environment, although the park includes a few Native American archaeological sites and isolated gold-extraction locations. The park's overwhelming significance is as a living laboratory of change. Plants and wildlife subsist here amid dynamic interactions of water, ice, and a glacier-carved landscape relentlessly pulled down by the Earth's crustal movements. The Harriman Expedition, a steamship-borne venture visiting the fjords in 1899, predicted this area's future value as a scenic tourist attraction. To protect this life and landscape, a national monument was proclaimed in 1978, and the Kenai Fjords National Park was established in 1980.

Kobuk Valley National Park

In the summer, grasses and grasslike sedges are eaten by caribou, which may be seen traversing the Kobuk Valley. (NATIONAL PARK SERVICE)

Located entirely north of the Arctic Circle, Kobuk Valley National Park is one of the most remote regions in the United States. Visitors are more likely to encounter Native Alaskans hunting migrating caribou than they are other tourists. The park embraces the central valley of the Kobuk River, and protects the rolling landscape of the 25-square-mile Great Kobuk Sand Dunes just south of the Kobuk River against the base of the Waring Mountains. In the northernmost reaches of the boreal forest, a rich array of arctic wildlife can be found, including caribou, grizzly and black bear, wolf, and fox.

Onion Portage and other significant archaeological sites reveal the layers of history of Native people who have lived along the Kobuk for 12,000 years. And fossils of Ice Age mammals have been preserved in the permafrost ice wedges in river bluffs. Composed of sand, the river bluffs can reach a spectacular 150 feet in height. The sand dunes are a remnant of the Ice Age – wind and water carried sand produced by the grinding of ancient glaciers to the Kobuk Valley, creating this Sahara-like landscape.

The Inupiaq people and other Native Alaskans still pursue the subsistence living of their ancestors – hunting caribou and fishing and trapping – while also relying on locally harvested animals, fish, and plants.

The caribou has a strong presence in Native stories of this region. Native peoples were often semi-nomadic, following the caribou migrations. The Kobuk River valley provides important fall and winter range for the western arctic caribou herds. Bands of bulls and cows may be seen here from late August through October as they cross the Kobuk River on their extensive annual migrations. The herd of caribou – more than 300,000 strong and North America's largest – travels northward to calving grounds on the Arctic Coastal Plain.

Traditionally, caribou have been among this region's chief food sources for humans, predators, and scavengers. The populations of some other animal species may even fluctuate with that of the caribou. Native peoples have depended on caribou for food; for shelter, using their hides to make tents; for clothing, such as coats, boots called "mukluks," trousers, and mittens; and for carving tools, using antler and bone for needles, sleigh brakes, fish spears, knife handles, arrowheads, hide scrapers, and snow shovels.

Caribou move about the tundra in constant search of vegetation to support their body weight – 150 to 300 pounds for bulls. The tundra offers a thin veneer of life. In summer the land is covered with a profusion of low-growing plants, including dwarfed ground willows, saxifrage, lupines, reindeer moss, and lichens. Caribou feed on grasses and grass-like sedges; small shrubs and their berries; and twigs and bark. In winter, they eat large quantities of reindeer moss. The caribou are prey for wolves and bears, some wolves following the caribou herd on its migratory route. Eagles attack vulnerable calves, and weasels, lemmings, some hawks, ravens, Canada jays, and gulls scavenge caribou carcasses.

Boaters may witness up close the impressive sight of caribou swimming across the Kobuk River. The river – up to 1,500 feet wide and nearly 300 miles long – placidly winds through the park, falling a mere 2 to 3 inches per mile before flowing into Hotham Inlet, and eventually the Chukchi Sea. With a current more like a calm lake's than a churning river's, the Kobuk can be an ideal setting for fishing. Bird-watchers may also identify more than 100 species of birds that flock here from across the Americas to breed in the summer. Hiking is for the truly adventurous – there are no trails here.

**KOBUK VALLEY
NATIONAL PARK
Established 1980
1,750,421 acres
P.O. Box 1029
Kotzebue, AK 99752
(907) 442-3760**

Lake Clark National Park and Preserve

The Alaska and Aleutian ranges join here, as clouds hug these awesome mountain peaks.
(NATIONAL PARK SERVICE)

The spectacular scenery of Lake Clark National Park and Preserve is unrivaled. Nestled in the heart of the Chigmit Mountains along the western shore of Cook Inlet, it contains great geologic diversity and ecosystems representative of the many regions of Alaska. Although continuously inhabited since early prehistoric times, the area remains wild and sparsely populated, with aircraft providing the primary means of access.

Within the park, the mountains of the Alaska and the Aleutian ranges join. The Chigmits, an awesome, jagged array of mountains, are the result of centuries of uplifting, intrusion, earthquakes, volcanism, and glacial action. Two symmetrical active volcanoes, Iliamna and Redoubt, form an important link in the Pacific chain of fire. Venting steam, snow-capped, and rising more than 10,000 feet, each is an impressive sight when viewed from the eastern side of the park.

The range's eastern flank descends rapidly to Cook Inlet. Rivers cascade dramatically to the sea through forests of Sitka and white spruce. The coastal cliffs, holding fossil remnants of 150 million years of sea life, are stark counterpoints to the active volcanoes and glacial streams that are reshaping the landscape. On marshes and outwash plains, swans and other waterfowl nest. The rocky cliffs in and adjacent to the park provide rookeries for puffins, cormorants, kittiwakes, and other seabirds. Seals and whales may occasionally be observed off shore.

The western flank of the Chigmit Mountains descends through tundra-covered foothills to boreal forest. Spectacular lakes and wild rivers fill the valleys, flowing southwestward to Bristol Bay. Fish include five species of salmon, rainbow trout, Dolly Varden trout, lake trout, northern pike, and arctic grayling. Dall's sheep, caribou, and moose forage the area. Brown and black bear are present, as well as wolves, lynx, foxes, and other mammals.

This western side of the park and preserve provides many recreational opportunities. Anglers find trophy fish; hikers explore high tundra slopes; river-runners thrill in the Tlikakila, Mulchatna, and Chilikadrotna wild rivers; and campers find lakeshore sites inspirational.

This vast area may also be harsh. Planning and preparing for a wilderness experience is critical to the enjoyment of the area in all conditions: wind, rain, snow, and sunshine.

Winter is long – October through April. In some locations the sun does not rise above the peaks for several months. A fresh snow can veil the area majestically, or winter winds may uncover a landscape of subtle brown highlighted by ice-blue frozen lakes. Breakup in spring can immobilize the area, as ice melts and frozen ground turns to mud. Summer is the time of life as caribou calve, buds turn to leaves, mosquitoes hatch, and salmon return to spawn. Clouds often cap the Chigmit Mountains and occasionally close the passes to aircraft. Precipitation is about a third less on the west side, but everywhere rain produces a summer floral display. Fireweed, lupine, blueberry, and bearberry abound. In autumn the burgundy-hued tundra blankets the slopes around aptly named Turquoise Lake. A light dusting of snow over the yellow birch and red bearberry produces a truly rare visual pleasure.

The area has been occupied since prehistoric times, and archaeological investigations are continuing to trace early settlement.

Janaina Indians lived at Kijik and Old Village until the early 1900s, when they moved to Nondalton and other sites. Russian explorers, traders, and missionaries began traversing the region in the 1790s. The salmon industry began attracting American and foreign settlers in the early 1900s. Around Lake Clark most were trappers and miners. Recent years have produced an economy based on subsistence lifestyles, commercial fishing, and recreation activities.

LAKE CLARK NATIONAL PARK AND PRESERVE
Established 1980
National park:
2,636,839 acres
National preserve:
1,407,293 acres
4230 University Drive,
Suite 311
Anchorage, AK 99508
(907) 781-2218

Lassen Volcanic National Park

Lassen Peak reflected in Lake Helen. At this high altitude, the ice and snow from the previous winter has not yet melted, even though this photo was taken in mid-September.

In May 1914, Lassen Peak eruped, beginning a seven-year cycle of sporadic volcanic outbursts. The climax of this extended episode took place in 1915, when the peak blew an enormous mushroom cloud some 7 miles skyward into the stratosphere. The reawakening of this volcano, which began as a vent on a larger extinct volcano known as "Tehama," profoundly altered the surrounding landscape.

The area was made a national park in 1916 because of its significance as an active volcanic landscape, other portions of which saw eruptions in 1851. The park is a compact laboratory of volcanic phenomena and most associated geothermal features, except true geysers. It is part of a vast geographic unit – a great lava plateau with isolated volcanic peaks – that also encompasses Lava Beds National Monument, in California, and Crater Lake National Park, in Oregon.

Before the 1980 eruption of Mount St. Helens in Washington, Lassen Peak was the most recent volcanic outburst in the contiguous forty-eight states. The peak is the southernmost volcano in the Cascade Range, which extends from here into Canada. The western part of the park features great lava pinnacles, huge mountains created by lava flows, jagged craters, and steaming sulphur vents. It is cut by spectacular glaciated canyons and is dotted and threaded with lakes and rushing clear streams. Snowbanks persist year-round, and beautiful meadows are spread with wildflowers in spring. The eastern part of the park is a vast lava plateau more than 1 mile above sea level. Here are found small cinder cones – Fairfield Peak, Hat Mountain, and Crater Butte. Forested with pine and fir, this area is studded with small lakes, but it boasts few streams. Warner Valley, marking the southern edge of the Lassen plateau, features hot-spring areas – Boiling Springs Lake, Devils Kitchen, and Terminal Geyser. This forested, steep valley also has gor-

LASSEN VOLCANIC NATIONAL PARK
Established 1916
106,372 acres
Mineral, CA 96063
(916) 595-4444

geous large meadows.

The 1980 eruption of Mount St. Helens reduced Lassen's superlative status, but it increased the park's significance as a sixty-five-year laboratory of possible recovery patterns for Mount St. Helens. The Devastated Area most visibly illustrates the slow but relentless return of Earth's green mantle of plants, with herbs, grasses, shrubs, and trees retaking the land. Many areas of the park are being reforested, with more variety of species than made up the mature forests that once stood on them. The apparent reason for such variety is lack of competition during the earlier stages of recovery. The park's plantlife mixes species of the Sierra Nevada to the south and of the Cascade Range with a relative abundance of some 715 plant species.

The Devastated Area evidences the combined mud-flow and gas-blast destruction typical of many volcanic eruptions in the Cascades. The Chaos Jumbles area looks similarly destroyed, but for a different reason. An air-cushioned avalanche – one that fell so rapidly en masse that it trapped and compressed air beneath itself – crashed down off the Chaos Crags about 300 years ago. The air acted as a lubricant, enabling the avalanche to rush across the valley at more than 100 miles per hour. It pushed 400 feet up the side of Table Mountain, before losing its momentum and surging back down across Manzanita Creek.

Lassen geothermal areas – Sulphur Works, Bumpass Hell (the largest), Little Hot Springs Valley, Boiling Springs Lake, Devils Kitchen, and Terminal Geyser – offer fumaroles, boiling mud pots, and waters above 212°F. Some of these thermal features are getting hotter. Scientists think that Lassen Park and Mount Shasta are the most likely candidates in the Cascades to join Mount St. Helens as active volcanoes.

The Lassen area was a meeting point for four Indian groups: Atsugewi, Yana, Yahi, and Maidu. These Native groups encamped here in warmer months for hunting and gathering. Basketmakers rather than potters, they have left few artifacts other than stone points, knives, and metates.

History here generally describes the period from 1840 on, even though mountain man Jedediah Smith passed through in 1828 on his overland trek to the West Coast. California's Gold Rush in 1848 brought the first settlers. Two pioneer trails, developed by William Nobles and Peter Lassen, are associated with the park. In 1851, Nobles discovered an alternative route to California, passing through Lassen. Sections of this Nobles Emigrant Trail are still visible in the park. Lassen, for whom the park is named, guided settlers near here and tried to found a city. Mining, power-development projects, ranching, and timbering were all attempted here. The area's early federal protection saved it from heavy logging.

Lassen Creek winds across Upper Meadow, below Lassen Peak.

Mammoth Cave National Park

From the beginning, underground explorers doubted that they would ever find the end of Mammoth Cave. Today, the cave still seems to be a wilderness without boundaries. The Mammoth Cave system goes on for more than 300 miles of known passages, and there is yet more cave to be explored. Lying beneath the Kentucky hills, it is the longest cave in the world. No other known cave even comes close.

In this vast subterranean world, there are giant vertical shafts, from the towering 192-foot-high Mammoth Dome to the 105-foot-deep Bottomless Pit. Some passages and rooms are decorated with sparkling white gypsum crystals, while others are filled with the colorful sculpted shapes of stalactites, stalagmites, and other cave formations. Underground rivers, with names like Echo River and the River Styx, flow through Mammoth's deepest chambers. And in the cave's absolute blackness dwell many rare and unusual animals, including eyeless fish, ghostly white spiders, and blind beetles.

Mammoth Cave is the centerpiece of one of the greatest cave regions in the world. The area, with its multitude of limestone caves, underground rivers, springs, and sinkholes, is known as a "karst" landscape. Water has been the guiding force in the creation of this landscape, including the intricate labyrinth of Mammoth. Underground water working in cracks and between rock layers has carved out Mammoth Cave's long, horizontal passageways over the past several million years. The upper passages, dry today, were hollowed out thousands of years ago; the lower passages are still being enlarged by the flowing waters of Echo River and other underground streams. Mammoth's huge vertical shafts, called "pits" and "domes," have been created by groundwater seeping downward through sinkholes or cracks located beyond the edge of the protective hard layer of sandstone that

The illuminated cave walls are decorated with glittering crystals, colored stalactites, stalagmites, and stunning cave formations. This cave system is the longest in the world. (NATIONAL PARK SERVICE)

overlies much of the cave. Water also has been essential in decorating parts of the cave with gypsum formations, stalactites, stalagmites, draperies, and flowstone. The delicate gypsum formations occur on the walls, ceilings, and floors of some of the cave's drier chambers; the rest of the formations appear in some of the wetter chambers. Since the creation of Mammoth

Cave, unusual fish, shrimp, crayfish, crickets, spiders, beetles, molds, and mushrooms have taken up residence in its protective environment of cool darkness. Many of the cave animals are blind, or nearly so, and some lack skin pigments as a result of living in the total blackness of the cave. Although sightless, many have other highly developed senses. Blind fish have extremely sensitive organs on the head and body that enable them to feel their way through the water. Cave crickets have exceptionally long antennae to perform essentially the same function on land. Other animals, such as bats and some cave salamanders, spend only part of their lives in the cave.

Since the days when prehistoric Indians explored the cave by the light of cane-reed torches, Mammoth has inspired the imagination, tested the courage, and awakened the senses of visitors. Ancient artifacts and well-preserved human mummies found in Mammoth indicate that people began venturing into the cave as early as 4,000 years ago. Modern-day encounters with the cave began, according to legend, in the

late 1790s, when a hunter chasing a bear through the hills near the Green River stumbled across its gaping entrance. This opening today is called "The Historic Entrance." At first just a curiosity,

**MAMMOTH CAVE
NATIONAL PARK
Established 1941
52,708 acres
Mammoth Cave, KY 42259
(502) 758-2328**

Mammoth became a valuable commercial property with the outbreak of the War of 1812 between the United States and England. Cave sediments with abundant quantities of nitrate, an essential

ingredient of gunpowder, were mined by slaves during the war. By the war's end, Mammoth was famous and soon became one of the nation's most popular attractions. Visitors came by stagecoach and by train to be led by guides through its mysterious subterranean world. "No ray of light but the glimmer of our lamps; no sound but the echo of our own steps; nothing but darkness, silence, immensity" is how one early visitor recalled his tour. Meanwhile, explorations were revealing more of Mammoth's wonders. Stephen Bishop, renowned guide and cave explorer, discovered miles of passages, underground rivers, and gypsum-decorated chambers in the mid-1800s. Later explorers followed

where Bishop left off, pushing the known extent of Mammoth even farther, or, like Kentucky farmer Floyd Collins, discovering other caves nearby. Meanwhile, extraordinary events took place in the cave. In the 1800s and early 1900s there were weddings, performances by Shakespearean actor Edwin Booth and singer Jenny Lind, and the establishment of a hospital for tuberculosis patients in the cave. At the same time, support was growing to protect Mammoth's natural wonders. Finally, in 1941, Mammoth Cave National Park was established to preserve its maze of passages, cavernous domes and pits, underground rivers and lakes, unusual animals, and beautiful navigable rivers and rugged topography.

Mesa Verde National Park

Pre-Columbian cliff dwellings and other works of the Anasazi are remarkably preserved in part of a large plateau rising high above the Montezuma and Mancos valleys. Mesa Verde National Park preserves a spectacular remnant of the 1,000-year-old culture of the Anasazi.

About 1,400 years ago, long before any European exploration of the New World, a group of Indians living in the Four Corners region chose Mesa Verde for their home. For over 700 years their descendants lived and flourished here, eventually building elaborate stone cities in the sheltered recesses of the canyon walls. Then, in the late 1200s, within the span of one or two generations, they abandoned their homes and moved away.

Ever since local cowboys discovered the cliff dwellings a century ago, archaeologists have been trying to understand the life of these people. But despite decades of excavation, analysis, classification, and comparison, our knowledge is still sketchy. We will never know the whole story of their existence, for they left no written records, and much that was important in their lives has perished. Yet for all their silence, these ruins speak with a certain eloquence. They tell of a people adept at building, artistic in their crafts, and skillful at wrestling a living from a difficult land. They are evidence of a society that over the centuries accumulated skills and traditions and passed them on from one generation to another. By classic times (A.D. 1100 to 1300), the Anasazi of Mesa Verde were the heirs of a vigorous civilization, with accomplishments in community living and the arts that rank among the finest expressions of human culture in ancient America.

Taking advantage of nature, the Anasazi built their dwellings under the overhanging cliffs. Their basic construction material was

The several dozen rooms of the Cliff Palace are all housed under a single huge rock overhang.

sandstone, which they shaped into rectangular blocks about the size of a loaf of bread. The mortar between the blocks was a mix of mud and water. Rooms averaged about 6 feet by 8, space enough for two or three persons. Isolated rooms in the rear and on the upper levels were generally used for storing crops.

Much of the daily routine took place in the open courtyards in front of the rooms. The women fashioned pottery there, while the men made various tools – knives, axes, awls, scrapers – out of stone and bone. The fires built in summer were mainly for cooking. In winter, when the alcove rooms were damp and uncomfortable, fires probably burned throughout the village. Smoke-blackened walls and ceilings are reminders of the biting cold these people lived with for half of the year.

Getting food was a ceaseless struggle, even in the best of years. Farming was the main business of these people, but they supplemented their crops of corn, beans, and squash by gathering wild plants and hunting deer, rabbits, squirrels, and other game. Their

only domestic animals were dogs and turkeys.

Fortunately for us, the Anasazi tossed their trash close by. Scraps of food, broken pottery and tools, anything unwanted went down the slope in front of their houses. Much of what we know about daily life here comes from these garbage heaps.

The first Anasazi settled in Mesa Verde (Spanish for "green table") about A.D. 550. They are known as basketmakers because of their impressive skill at that craft. Formerly a nomadic people, they were now beginning to lead a more settled way of life. Farming replaced hunting and gathering as their main source of livelihood. They lived in pithouses clustered into small villages, which they usually built on the mesa tops but occasionally in the cliff recesses. They soon learned how to make pottery, and they acquired the bow and arrow, a more efficient weapon for hunting than the *atlatl*, or spear-thrower.

These were fairly prosperous times for the basketmakers, and the population multiplied. About 750 they began building houses above ground, with upright walls

made of poles and mud. From this time on, these people are known as "Pueblos," a Spanish word for "village dwellers."

By 1000, the Anasazi had advanced from pole-and-adobe construction to skillful stone masonry. Pottery also changed, as black drawings on a white background replaced crude designs on dull gray. Farming provided more of the diet than before.

MESA VERDE NATIONAL PARK
Established 1906
52,122 acres
Mesa Verde National Park, CO
81321
(303) 529-4461

The years from 1100 to 1300 were Mesa Verde's classic period. The population may have reached several thousand. It was mostly concentrated in compact villages of many rooms, often with kivas built inside the enclosing walls rather than out in the open. Round towers began to appear, and there was a rising level of craftsmanship in masonry work,

pottery, weaving, jewelry, and even tool-making. About 1200 there was another major population shift. The Anasazi began to move back into the cliff alcoves that had sheltered their ancestors. We don't know why they made this move. Perhaps it was for defense; perhaps the caves offered better protection from the elements; perhaps there were religious or psychological reasons. Whatever prompted the move, it gave rise to the cliff dwellings for which Mesa Verde is famous.

The Anasazi lived in the cliff houses for less than 100 years. By 1300, Mesa Verde was deserted. Here is another mystery. We know that the last quarter of the century was a time of drought and crop failures. Maybe after hundreds of years of intensive use, the land and its resources – the soil, forests, and animals – were depleted.

When the Anasazi left, they may have traveled south into New Mexico and Arizona, perhaps settling among their kin already there. Whatever happened, it seems likely that some Pueblo Indians today are descendants of the cliff-dwellers of Mesa Verde.

Mount Rainier National Park

The peak of Mount Rainier is mirrored in Tipsoo Lake at sunrise.

The glacial peaks of Mount Rainier are visible long before one reaches the park. Nearly 3 miles high, Mount Rainer is the loftiest volcanic peak of the Cascade Range. Mount Rainier, a landscape of dense forests, wildflowers, tremendous snowfields, and rugged glaciers, was created by fire and ice. The mountain is a volcano born of fire and built up above the surrounding country by repeated eruptions and successive flows of lava. It is a relatively young volcano, only about 1 million years old. By contrast the mountains of the Cascade Range that Mount Rainier looks down upon are at least 12 million years old, created by the folding, buckling, and uplifting of the Earth's surface. Mount Rainier is not an isolated volcano, for from Lassen Peak, in California, to Mount Garibaldi, in British Columbia, an entire line of volcanoes defines the north–south march of the Cascades. These peaks dominate the skyline, ever a reminder that they are only dormant and may at any time, like Lassen Peak in 1914–21 and Mount St. Helens in 1980, erupt in fury and rage at the fragile world built by humans.

One of the unexpected side benefits of these eruptions has been the deposition of ash and pumice layers that are rich in nutrients and support the abundance of wildflowers throughout the mountainous Pacific Northwest. Even as volcanic forces were building up this land, the slow, inevitable power of glacial ice began to shape and form it. Glaciers come from the snow that does not melt from year to year: it accumulates to greater and greater depths. Pressing the air out, the weight of the snow packs it down tight and compresses it into ice. Gravity pulls the ice down the mountainside, both scouring and smoothing the bedrock as it goes. Freezing and thawing break rocks from the adjacent slopes, and they fall onto the glacier's surface. More debris is picked up by the passing ice. This is an inexorable process that continues today and will alter the mountain in the tomorrows to come.

The highest point in the park reached by road is Sunrise, at 6,400 feet. From here the views of Emmons Glacier, the largest on Mount Rainier, are breathtaking. On very clear days, this is also the spot for views of some of the other volcanoes in the Cascades Range.

Mount Rainier's roads and more than 300 miles of trails lead through spectacular mountain scenery – from the old-growth forest and up into the subalpine areas. The subalpine meadow called "Paradise" is a major point from which to begin a hike. When Elcaine Longmire's wife first saw

MOUNT RAINIER NATIONAL PARK
Established 1899
235,404 acres
Tahoma Woods, Star Route
Ashford, WA 98304
(206) 569-2211

this meadow, she exclaimed, "It looks just like paradise!" With its view of Mount Rainier in the distance, the meadows and forests in the foreground, and the clear mountain air all around, Paradise is well named. Having an average of 620 inches of snow falling each winter, Paradise is an ideal location for such winter activities as snowshoeing, cross-country skiing, and "tubing."

In Ohanapecosh, the lowland forest reigns supreme and reaches its true glory in the Grove of the Patriarchs. Here Douglas fir, western red cedar, and western hemlock rival the grandeur of the coastal redwood forests in California and Oregon.

The heaviest rainfall and most luxuriant forest exist in the park's northwest corner in Carbon River, which was named for the coal deposits found in the area. Some botanists suggest that rather than a lowland forest, what is found here is an example of a temperate rain forest.

The seasons and elevation play a large role in determining where to find the best wildlife. In summer, chipmunks, chickarees, ground squirrels, marmots, and pika are commonly seen mammals; Steller's jays, gray jays, Clark's nutcrackers, and ravens are commonly noticed birds. Deer are frequently seen, but elk, black bear, and mountain goats are more elusive. Elk can be spotted on the east side of the park in September. To see a black bear, which may be brown, tan, or blond in color, is a rare treat. Mountain goats stay close to high country cliffs.

The park's oldest developed area is Longmire, the site of Mineral Spring Resort, which James Longmire opened in 1884. After the park was established in 1899, Longmire became the park headquarters. Today the original administrative building houses a museum that tells the story of those early days. The drive from Nisqually Entrance to Longmire takes you on one of the world's most beautiful forest roads.

A sprinkling of wildflowers amid the rocks above the timberline.

North Cascades National Park

A panorama of characteristically jagged peaks from high above Cascade Pass.

The lofty jagged peaks of the Cascades rank among the world's great mountain ranges, often called the American Alps. "Nowhere do the mountain masses and peaks present such strange, fantastic, dauntless and startling outlines as here," wrote Henry Custer. He worked his way through the North Cascades as assistant of reconnaissances for the International Boundary Commission in 1859. Custer was the first to extol this region in writing but admitted that words failed him. More than 100 years later, the area became parkland with the establishment of North Cascades National Park, and Ross Lake and Lake Chelan national recreation areas, in 1968. In 1988, Congress designated approximately 92 percent of the three areas as the Stephen Mather Wilderness to provide additional legislated protection.

The Cascades, extending from Canada's Fraser River south beyond Oregon, contribute greatly to shaping the Pacific Northwest's climate and vegetation. These three national park system areas sit deep in the wild, nearly impenetrable northernmost reaches of the Cascade Range in northwestern Washington. This land stretches from rich lowland valleys through dense forests to the tops of glacier-covered peaks, then back down to the arid eastern slopes. The diversity of environments allows a corresponding profusion of different kinds of plants and animals.

North Cascades National Park contains some of America's most breathtakingly beautiful scenery – high jagged peaks, ridges, slopes, and countless cascading waterfalls. The park encompasses some 318 glaciers, more than half of all glaciers in the contiguous United States. Hiking, backpacking, and mountaineering are the most popular activities in the park. Road access is limited, but views into the park can be had on clear days from the North Cascades Highway at Goodell Creek, Diablo Lake Overlook, and other places. The Cascade River Road – 25 miles of improved dirt and gravel

– gives summer and fall access into the park and to the Cascade Pass Trailhead.

**NORTH CASCADES
NATIONAL PARK
Established 1968
504,781 acres
2105 Highway 20
Sedro Woolley, WA 98284
(206) 856-5700**

From many park trails, endless views unfold of glacially sculpted valleys, glaciers, and snowfields. Rumbling sounds frequently interrupt the subalpine stillness as icefalls crash into the valley floor. At Cascade Pass, over which Alexander Ross, an early explorer of this region, is presumed to have traveled, flower-sprinkled hillsides and meadows enhance spectacular views of the Cascade and Stehekin valleys. Here, as at other passes and high-elevation viewpoints, you can best see the rock ridges, glaciers, snowfields, cascading waterfalls, and other alpine and subalpine features against their backdrops of sky.

Within the three national park system areas, more than 1,500 different species of plants have been identified, along with hundreds of birds, reptiles, and amphibians, and thousands of insects. While not abundant, bears, wolves, mountain lions, falcons, and bald eagles also add to the genetic richness of the area.

Few people were familiar with this area before the parklands were established. Recent historic exploration began in 1814, when Alexander Ross crossed the current national park's southern unit. The handful of explorers who followed Ross also commented on the region's rugged, isolated nature.

Miners prospected for gold, lead, zinc, and platinum here from 1880 to 1910. They recorded moderate strikes, but transportation proved to be arduous and profits so limited that mining was abandoned. Some logging and homesteading occurred around 1900. The electricity-generating potential of the Skagit River was early recognized. Between 1924 and 1961, Seattle City Light built three dams on the river.

Mountains do not stop at the park boundaries. The three areas are flanked on the south, east, and west by national forest lands, and on the north by provincial lands of British Columbia, Canada. The national forest lands encompass a number of outstanding federal wilderness areas, including the Glacier Peak Wilderness on the Mt. Baker–Snoqualmie and Wenatchee national forests. Only an invisible boundary separates the two national park units from the two national recreation areas and the adjoining national forest lands.

Evidence of Indian use of the Cascades is widespread, but little is known about it. Readily reached areas are heavily visited now, but some remote locations have yet to feel the boots of today's back-country traveler. Forest giants of western red cedar and Douglas fir dot the deep valleys. Off the trail, tangled growths of alder, vine maple, stinging nettles, and devil's club still defy cross-country hikers. Glaciers scored by crevasses, permanent snowfields, sheer-walled cliffs, spires, and pinnacles challenge the mountaineer.

Olympic National Park

In Washington's Olympic Peninsula lies Olympic National Park, a diverse and stunning landscape – fog-shrouded coast, with booming surf and wave-manicured beaches; spectacular alpine country, dotted with sparkling lakes, lush meadows, and glaciers; and North America's finest temperate rain forest.

The 57-mile-long coastline of Olympic National Park has remained little changed over time, except for the impact of the pounding surf and storms upon the mainland. The coastline looks much as it did when early Indians built their first villages on these shores, thousands of years before European explorers arrived.

The coast is where the land meets the sea, vibrating with life and energy. Drift logs cast high on the beach; sculptured arches and sea stacks; the roar of crashing waves; the calls of gulls, bald

Western red cedar is one of several species of trees that reach record size in the park's rain forest.

eagles, and black oystercatchers; three-dimensional clouds; dramatic sunsets; the sheer vastness of the ocean; and myriad other elements draw visitors to this wilderness. The coast is inhabited by numerous shorebirds, and a host of other creatures – from raccoons that feed on shellfish to bear, deer, and river otters.

The forests of Olympic National Park boast several species of trees that reach record sizes. The forest canopy is so thick in some locations that falling snow is caught in the trees and never reaches the ground. There are four basic types of forests on the Olympic peninsula: temperate rain forest, lowland, montane, and subalpine.

Temperate rain forests are rare. They can be found only in New Zealand, southern Chile, and here on the northwest coast of the United States in the valleys of the Quinault, Queets, and Hoh rivers. What defines a rain forest is quite simply rain – lots of it. On the

OLYMPIC NATIONAL PARK
Established 1938
922,651 acres
600 East Park Avenue
Port Angeles, WA 98362
(206) 452-4501

Olympic coast precipitation averages 145 inches, more than 12 feet, every year. The mountains to the east also protect the coastal areas from severe weather extremes. Seldom does the temperature drop below freezing in the rain forest, and summertime highs rarely exceed 80°F. The dominant species in the rain forest are Sitka spruce and western hemlock; some grow to tremendous size, reaching 300 feet in height and 23 feet in circumference. Douglas fir, western red cedar, bigleaf maple, red alder, vine maple, and black cottonwood are also found throughout the forest.

Lying above the temperate rain forest is the lowland forest. Western hemlock is probably the most common tree here, although stands of Douglas fir may prevail where fire or drier conditions caused by the rain shadow give them an advantage. The lowland forest gives way to the montane forest, where silver fir grows. As the elevation increases, the subalpine landscape of subalpine fir, mountain hemlock, or Alaska cedar appears. Delightful alpine meadows graced with wildflowers and glacial lakes often intermingle here with stands of firs. From seashore to mountaintop, Olympic is blessed with a rich plant community created by varying environments.

The Olympic Mountains are not very high – Mount Olympus, the highest, is just under 8,000 feet – but they rise almost from the water's edge and intercept moisture-rich air masses that move in from the Pacific. As this air is forced over the mountains, it cools and releases precipitation in the form of rain or snow. At lower elevations, rain nurtures the forests, while at higher elevations, snow adds to glacial masses that relentlessly carve the landscape.

These mountains arose from the sea some 35 million years ago, when the Pacific Ocean floor containing huge underwater mountains crashed against the North American mainland. Most of the sea floor went beneath the continental land mass, but some of the sea floor was scraped off and jammed against the mainland, creating the dome that would become today's Olympics. Powerful forces fractured, folded, and overturned rock formations, which helps explain the jumbled appearance of the Olympics.

Surrounded on three sides by water and still crowned by alpine glaciers, the Olympics retain the distinctive character that developed from their isolation. Several plants and animals are unique to the Olympics – examples of how genetic diversification occurs when geographical isolation exits. The most striking example is the Olympic marmot, with its distinct chromosomal and behavioral patterns. Others include Flett's violet, Piper's bellflower, Olympic Mountain daisy, Olympic chipmunk, Olympic snow mole, and Beardslee and Crescenti trout.

People have lived here for

Alpine wildflowers, mule deer, and mountain panoramas can often be seen together at Hurricane Ridge.

thousands of years, but the earliest inhabitants lived primarily along the coast, taking food from the sea, and berries, roots, and meat from the land. From the nearby forests they cut cedars that provided hulls for their canoes, building materials for their lodges, and many of the miscellaneous items of everyday life.

The first European – Juan de Fuca – may have come to these shores in 1592. Reliable evidence of European penetration is not available until 1774, when Juan Perez sailed along this coast. In the next twenty-five years, British, American, and Spanish explorers visited the area. The most enduring work was done by Robert Gray, an American, and George Vancouver, an Englishman. Both men explored the area thoroughly, establishing rival claims to this land for their own countries. Not until 1885, when Lieutenant Joseph P. O'Neil led the first documented expedition, was any real attempt made to explore the interior of the Olympic Peninsula. Slowly a movement got under way to preserve the peninsula, which was eventually set aside as national park in 1938.

Intertidal life amid the sea stacks at the north end of the coastal section of the park.

Sea stacks and surf after sunset near La Push.

Petrified Forest National Park

At Tiponi Point, cloud shadows play across the colored ground of the Painted Desert.

The strong desert sun highlights the brilliant hues of petrified wood strewn across this arid tableland of northeastern Arizona. The crystalline patterns of the petrified wood were created millions of years ago when dinosaurs roamed what was then a vast floodplain. Tall, stately pine-like trees grew along the headwaters. Crocodile-like reptiles; giant, fish-eating amphibians; and small dinosaurs lived among a variety of ferns, cycads, and other plants and animals that are known only as fossils today. The tall trees – Araucarioxylon, Woodworthia, and Schilderia – fell and were washed by swollen streams into the floodplain. There they were covered by silt, mud, and volcanic ash, and this blanket of deposits cut off oxygen and slowed the logs' decay. Gradually silica-bearing groundwater seeped through the logs and, bit by bit, encased the original wood tissues with silica deposits. Slowly the process continued, the silica crystallized into the quartz, and the logs were preserved as petrified wood.

That was about 225 million years ago, in the late Triassic. Later, the area sank, was flooded, and was covered with freshwater sediments. The area was lifted far above sea level, and this uplift created stresses that cracked the giant logs. In recent geological time, wind and water wore away the accumulated layers of hardened sediments, exposing the petrified logs and fossilized animal and plant remains on the Painted Desert landscape.

Today the ever-present forces of wind and water continue to remove sediments. Erosion continues to break down the giant logs and to reach for the remaining fossils still buried below the surface. In some places, up to 300 feet of fossil-bearing material remains. The petrified logs, the other fossils of plants and creatures that lived in the area, the rocks locking them in place – all testify to changes in the environment through millions of years.

Indian ruins, petroglyphs, and other sites throughout the park remain as evidence of human habitation in the area for more than 2,000 years. Excavated and partially restored rooms at the Puerco Indian Ruin are silent testimony to the people who lived here before A.D. 1400. An overlook, with telescopes, permits views of Newspaper Rock, a huge sandstone block covered with petro-

PETRIFIED FOREST NATIONAL PARK
Established 1962
93,533 acres
P.O. Box 2217
Petrified Forest National Park, AZ 86028
(602) 524-6228

glyphs. The complete history of this region is unknown, but evidence exists of separate occupations, a cultural transition from wandering families to settled agricultural villages (pueblos), and trading ties with neighboring villages. The Anasazi carved weapons and tools out of the petrified wood, and used the rock gems for trade.

This story of early people, told by potsherds, rubble, and pictures on the rocks, fades about A.D. 1400.

U.S. Army mappers and surveyors first came across the Painted Desert and pocketed the remarkable petrified wood in the mid-1800s. Farmers, ranchers, and sightseers then made their way into the area, rushing to collect the wood as souvenirs, or to create jewelry, clocks, furniture, and other decorative objects with the polished quartz rock. After a period of using the wood for souvenirs and numerous commercial ventures, residents recognized that the supply of petrified wood was not endless. In 1906 selected "forests" were set aside as Petrified Forest National Monument. In 1932 some 2,500 acres more of the Painted Desert were purchased and added to the monument, and in 1962 Petrified Forest National Park was established. Strict regulations forbid visitors to remove any rock from the park, but petrified wood can be bought from commercial dealers who collect it from areas outside the park.

Redwood National Park

The world's tallest living thing, the redwood tree, is a living link to the Age of Dinosaurs. It grows from a seed the size of a tomato seed and may reach 500 tons and stand taller than the Statue of Liberty. Acquiring its thick biological armor of umber bark, this tree seems impenetrable to the ravages of fire and insects. But the redwoods could not protect themselves from logging at the turn of the century.

When Friar Juan Crespi, who named the tree *palo colorado*, "red tree," saw the redwood forests in 1769, they probably covered 2 million or more acres. By 1965, they were reduced to 300,000 acres and were under intense logging pressure. When gold fever subsided here, redwood fever replaced it. At first, the forests seemed endless, but most of them fell to private ownership. Modern logging meth-

Columns of wood surround cathedral-like spaces along the trails through Lady Bird Johnson Grove.

ods raised the specter that all the trees might be cut. The State of California had preserved several groves before 1968, when Congress created Redwood National Park. Congress expanded the park in 1978 and directed the National Park Service to rehabilitate land that had been overlogged. Coast redwood, Douglas fir, and other native trees are planted to redevelop forests similar to those cut. Reshaping logging roads prevents erosion that clogs Redwood Creek and endangers stream-side trees. Congress also created a Park Protection Zone – 30,000 acres upstream from the park, in Redwood Creek – to limit effects of timber harvest on the park downstream. Today redwoods grow in a narrow strip along the Pacific Coast of California and southwestern Oregon.

Coast redwoods tower over all other trees in the world. At 367.8 feet, a coast redwood discovered on the banks of Redwood Creek in 1963 is known as the world's tallest tree. Located on the Sierra Nevada's west slope, giant sequoias, the cousins of redwoods, grow larger in diameter and bulk, but not in

height. Coast redwoods survive to be about 2,000 years old, averaging 500 to 700 years old.

Though the tree was named by Crespi, botanical credit for the coast redwood's discovery is generally ceded to Archibald Menzies, who noted it in 1794. In 1847 it was given its scientific name, *Sequoia sempervirens* (*sempervirens* means "evergreen"), probably honoring Cherokee leader Sequoyah.

The northern or redwood coast of California was largely ignored by Spaniards and Anglos until the Gold Rush. In 1850, gold was discovered on Gold Bluffs Beach. Mining proved marginally profitable. Revived during the Civil War, mines closed again at its end. Various methods were tried in the 1870s through the 1890s, but operations ceased by 1920. Remains of mining operations still exist on Gold Bluffs.

Logging began in redwood country in 1851. At first small logs were floated to small mills or dragged by oxen on skid roads. The railroad came into use in the 1870s, followed by the steam donkey in 1882, and the bull donkey ten years later. Bulldozers were

used by the 1920s, and trucks by the 1940s. Redwood lumber was used to build some of San Francisco's great Victorian homes.

Apart from its majestic redwoods, the park's wildlife also merits protection. From sea level to 3,100 feet in elevation in the Coast Range, a mild, moist climate

REDWOOD NATIONAL PARK
Established 1968
110,232 acres
1111 Second Street
Crescent City, CA 95531
(707) 464-6101

assures the park an abundant diversity of wildlife. Elusive to visitors, many species of mammals, birds, amphibians, and insects inhabit the mature redwood forest, depending on it for food and shelter. Seldom seen, black bears number several hundred in the park. They favor the recently logged Redwood Creek area, whose revegetation fosters abundant food. Prairies, called "bald hills," form natural islands of grasslands, where wildlife abounds. In spring-

time, prairie wildflowers burst with color that gives way in the dry summer to the grasslands' amber glow. Prairies are the realm of raptors, the predatory red-tailed hawk, kestrel, and great horned owl, and their prey of gophers and meadow mice. Mountain lions, bobcats, coyotes, foxes, elk, and black-tailed deer also frequent prairies, which were historically kept free of trees by wildfire and elk. Acorn-bearing Oregon white oaks edge prairies at higher elevations. They provided protein-rich food for Indians, who cleared their understory with fire. Prairies make good birding spots, where goldfinches, juncoes, quail, or ravens may be spotted.

The park's rivers are home to the sleek and graceful river otter. The Smith River, named for mountain man Jedediah Smith, arises in the Siskiyou Mountains and flows through the park's north section. It is California's last major free-flowing river, and it is famous for salmon and steelhead. The salmon and steelhead resources of Redwood Creek, which flows through the park's southern section, have been severely dimin-

ished by logging activities within its watershed.

Redwood National Park's rugged coastline, with stretches of steep, rocky cliffs broken by rolling slopes, is largely unaltered by humans. Generally rocky, its tidal zone can be difficult to traverse, with exceptions such as Gold Bluffs Beach, a 7-mile stretch of dunes and sandy beach. The coast offers a rich mix of life forms. Many of the park's marine bird species are migratory. Brown pelicans are summer visitors, cormorants take to lagoon or river and shore waters, and willets and sanderlings work the beach. Offshore may be seen California gray whales in migration, seals, sea lions, dolphins, porpoises, and orca (killer) whales.

LEFT: Sea mist commonly nourishes the coastal redwood groves during the warmer days of the year.

RIGHT: The redwood forest contains the greatest amount of biomass per unit area of any environment on earth.

Rocky Mountain National Park

Longs Peak from the highest point (over 12,000 feet above sea level) along Trail Ridge Road.

The snow-mantled peaks of Rocky Mountain National Park rise above verdant subalpine valleys and glistening lakes. One-third of the park is above the tree line, and here tundra predominates – a major reason why these peaks and valleys have been set aside as a national park.

Indians inhabited this area at least 1,000 years ago. As recently as the past two centuries, the Utes, and later the Arapahoes, lived off this rich land. The first Europeans to see this area were French fur traders. Miners were attracted to the area in the late nineteenth century by silver and gold. In 1859, Joel Estes and his son, Milton, rode into the valley that bears their name. Few others settled in this rugged country, and about 1909, Enos Mills, a naturalist, writer, and conservationist, began to campaign for preservation of this pristine area. Mills's campaign succeeded, and the area became Rocky Mountain National Park in 1915. Today, the park is easily accessible, only two hours' drive from Denver.

The park is characterized by marked differences found with the changing elevation. At lower levels, in the foothills and mountain ecosystem, open stands of ponderosa pine and juniper grow on the slopes facing the sun; on cooler north slopes are Douglas fir. Gracing the stream sides are blue spruces intermixed with dense stands of lodgepole pine. Here and there appear groves of aspen. Wildflowers dot meadows and glades. Higher still, forests of Englemann spruce and subalpine fir take over in the subalpine ecosystem. Openings in these cool, dark forests produce wildflower gardens of rare beauty and luxuriance, where the blue Colorado columbine reigns. At the upper edges of this zone, the trees are twisted and grotesque, and hug the ground. Then the trees disappear and you are in alpine tundra – a

ROCKY MOUNTAIN NATIONAL PARK
Established 1915
265,727 acres
Estes Park, CO 80517
(303) 586-2371

harsh, fragile world. In this flower-rich meadowland, more than one-quarter of the plants can also be found in the Arctic. The tundra's growing season is very short – sometimes less than ten weeks. Five-year-old plants are sometimes smaller than the end of your finger. The tundra is a delicate ecosystem, and recovery from severe damage may take several hundred years.

Many small mammals are easily seen in Rocky Mountain National Park, but larger animals such as wapiti (elk) and deer are generally seen at dawn or in late evening.

Bighorns – the living symbol of Rocky Mountain National Park – venture out at midday into Horseshoe Park, near Sheep Lakes, where there is a natural mineral lick. The gray jay may also be seen, often perching on a blue spruce. The wild, eerie, yipping song of the coyote is familiar on fall and winter evenings at Moraine Park and Horseshoe Park. Beaver, which are common in many streams, are often easy to find around their ponds and lodges in the evening. They usually begin working at sunset and continue long after dark. Above the tree line, in the alpine tundra, the yellow-bellied marmot suns itself on the rocks.

The Trail Ridge Road leading into the park is one of the great alpine highways in the United States. It crosses the park from east to west and then drops into the

Kawuneeche Valley, where the North Fork of the Colorado River flows. The road's winding course takes you 12,183 feet above sea level and into a world akin to the arctic regions.

Recreational activities in the park range from horseback riding, hiking, climbing, and fishing to cross-country skiing in the lower valleys and winter mountaineering in the high country. In the mountain streams and lakes of Rocky Mountain National Park, fishers can hook four species of trout: German brown, rainbow, brook, and cutthroat. The park maintains more than 260 miles of horseback-riding trails, and visitors can hire horses and guides to explore the park. Along numerous trails, hikers can escape the crowds and savor the streams, meadows, and mountains in remote sections of the park.

Saguaro National Park

The saguaro has been described as the monarch of the Sonoran Desert, as a prickly horror, as the supreme symbol of the American Southwest, and as a plant with personality. It is renowned for the variety of odd, all-too-human shapes it assumes, shapes that inspire wild and fanciful imaginings. Since 1933 this extraordinary giant cactus has been protected within what was formerly Saguaro National Monument. Consisting of two districts, Saguaro West and Saguaro East, and separated by the city of Tucson, the area was made a national park in 1994. Preserved along with it are many of the other members of the Sonoran Desert community – the other cacti, the desert trees and shrubs, and the animals. In lushness and variety of life, the Sonoran Desert far surpasses all other North American deserts. And yet, paradoxically, it is one of the hottest and driest regions on the continent. Summer midday temperatures quite commonly climb above 100°F. Less than 12 inches of rain fall in a

typical year. Between the summer and winter rainy seasons, it is not unusual for months to pass without a drop of rain. The plants and animals able to survive in this environment, with adaptations specially designed for desert survival, make up one of the most interesting and unusual collections of life in the United States.

A variety of plants live in the Sonoran Desert with the saguaro. There are more than fifty types of cacti, including hedgehog cactus, barrel cactus, fishhook cactus, teddybear cholla, and pricklypear, all of which, like the saguaro, are adapted to extreme heat and drought. There is creosote bush, the most widespread of all North American desert plants, and mesquite, a common desert tree. The ocotillo, which sprouts leaves within days after a rainstorm, only to drop them as moisture disappears, grows here, too, as does the

In the Tucson Mountains, the cacti are big enough and numerous enough to deserve the description "saguaro forest."

paloverde, with its small moisture-saving leaves. Annual flowers, such as the desert marigold, bloom in spring or summer, when conditions are right. Although the desert community predominates in Saguaro National Park, woodlands and forests grow on higher mountain slopes.

Desert animals are well adapted to life in their demanding environment. Many avoid the heat of day by venturing out only at night. These nocturnal animals include the cactus mouse and western diamondback rattlesnake. Other creatures restrict their activities to cooler morning and evening hours. Gambel's quail, road-runners, and other birds feed at these times, as do many reptiles, including the desert tortoise and Gila monster. Animals who are out at midday have special adaptations for dissipating heat. One such animal, the jackrabbit, radiates heat from its oversized ears. Desert creatures also have ways of dealing with the acute shortage of water. During droughts, javelinas eat succulent pricklypear pads. The kangaroo rat never needs to drink a drop of water, getting all it needs

from the seeds it eats. Some animals, like the cactus wren, use desert plants to their advantage. This bird builds its nest in the spiny cholla, where its nestlings are well protected.

SAGUARO NATIONAL PARK
Established 1994
19,061 acres
3693 South Old Spanish Trail
Tucson, AZ 85730
(602) 296-8576

The saguaro is like a multi-storied apartment complex: many animals live in close quarters, and the occupants change constantly. Two common residents are the Gila woodpecker and gilded flicker. These birds dwell in nest holes they excavate in the trunk and larger branches of saguaros. The birds make new nest holes each spring, and they often make and reject several cavities in one nesting season before settling in one and raising a family. Their industriousness leaves many holes for other animals, who are quick to move in. The birds who compete

for the homes include sparrow hawks, or American kestrel, Lucy's warblers, cactus wrens, western kingbirds, phainopeplas, elf owls, screech owls, and purple martins. Honeybees also inhabit some holes. For residents, the holes are a retreat from desert temperature extremes. Well insulated by thick walls, the holes are as much as 20°F cooler in summer and 20°F warmer in winter than outside. Other saguaro dwellers live not in holes but in bulky nests. These include red-tailed hawks and Harris hawks.

A saguaro's growth is extremely slow. After 15 years, the saguaro may be barely a foot tall. At about 30 years, saguaros begin to flower and produce fruit. By 50 years, the cactus can be as tall as 7 feet. After about 75 years, it may sprout its first branches, or "arms." The branches begin as prickly balls, then extend out and upward.

By 100 years, the saguaro may have reached 25 feet. Saguaros that live 150 years or more attain the grandest sizes, towering as high as 50 feet and weighing 8 tons – and sometimes more – dwarfing every other living thing in the desert.

These are the largest cacti in the United States. Their huge bulk is supported by a strong but flexible cylinder-shaped framework of long woody ribs.

In some forests of Saguaro National Park, deaths have greatly outnumbered the growth of new young saguaros. Biologists believe killing freezes are the major cause of saguaro deaths in the park. The saguaros here are at the extreme northern and eastern edge of their range, where the coldest winter temperatures most often occur. Humans, too, have played a part in the decline. Livestock grazing, which continued from the 1880s until 1979, devastated some cactus forests. Many seedlings were killed outright by trampling or were unable to find suitable places to grow because the ground had been compacted, and nurse plants killed.

Today, with grazing eliminated, recovery appears to be under way in several areas, where thousands of young saguaros have taken hold and are thriving. Still, natural forces, vandalism, and cactus rustling – the theft of saguaros for use in landscaping – continue to take a toll on the park's saguaro forests.

Sequoia and Kings Canyon National Parks

Sequoia National Park is home to the Earth's largest living thing – the General Sherman giant sequoia tree. In cathedral-like Giant Forest, named by the pioneering conservationist John Muir, stands the 275-foot-tall tree, whose trunk weighs an estimated 1,385 tons and whose circumference at the ground is nearly 103 feet. At least one tree species lives longer than the giant sequoia, one has a greater diameter, and three grow taller, but none has more volume.

"When I entered this sublime wilderness the day was nearly done," observed Muir; "the trees with rosy, glowing countenances seemed to be hushed and thoughtful, as if waiting in conscious religious dependence on the sun, and one naturally walked softly and awe-stricken among them."

Countless visitors have walked in Muir's footsteps to marvel at the giant sequoias, which, in all the

Sequoias don't die of old age, and they are fiercely resistant to fire and insect damage.

world, grow naturally only in some seventy-five groves on the west slopes of California's Sierra Nevadas. The giant sequoia has a column-like trunk, huge stout branches, and cinnamon-colored bark. Also called "Sierra redwood" and "Big Tree," it has the scientific name *Sequoiadendron giganteum*. The taller and more slender coast redwood, *Sequoia sempervirens*, is more conifer-like in profile and grows naturally only in a narrow strip along the Pacific Coast.

Sequoias do not die of old age, and they are fiercely resistant to fire and insect damage. "Most of the Sierra trees die of disease, fungi," Muir wrote, "but nothing hurts the Big Tree. Barring accidents, it seems to be immortal." Muir was partially right. The General Sherman Tree is between 2,300 and 2,700 years old. Chemicals in the wood and bark provide resistance to insects and fungi. The main cause of death for sequoias is toppling, as the trees have a shallow root system with no taproot. Soil moisture, root damage, and strong winds can also lead to toppling.

Sequoia National Park was created in 1890, after San Joaquin Valley residents and others pressed Congress to protect Sierra tracts against logging in the 1880s. Some park proponents sought to protect water supplies for irrigation; others, the Big Trees. Preserving land for scenic and recreational values was an infant idea then. Kings Canyon National Park, created in 1940, has been managed jointly with Sequoia National Park since 1943.

Steep and barren, the parks' canyon areas seem skeletal and cut to their geologic quicks. Kings Canyon reaches a depth outside the park of some 8,200 feet, from river level up to Spanish Mountain's peak. There, just downstream from the confluence of the Middle and South forks of the Kings River, the canyon is without peer in North America – deeper than the Snake River's Hells Canyon, in Idaho, and the Grand Canyon, in Arizona. Kern Canyon, in southern Sequoia National Park, is 6,000 feet deep, and several

other canyons exceed 4,000 feet in depth. Sierran canyons show both stream-cut, V-shaped profiles, and U-shaped profiles characteristic of glacial gouging.

The Sierra Nevada – more than 400 miles long and 60 to 80 miles wide – exceeds the whole Alps area – French, Swiss, and Italian. Palisade Crest in Kings Canyon National Park and the Mount Whitney group in Sequoia each boast six peaks over 14,000 feet in elevation.

No roads cross the range here; intimate appreciations of the mountains' scale and grandeur are hard-won afoot. Panoramic vistas can be seen by roadside pullouts and from atop Moro Rock, a dome-shaped granite monolith. To the north of Moro Rock lies the Giant Forest plateau, where sequoias rise above their forest neighbors. To the west, in contrast to these gargantuan conifers, are the dry foothills, with their oak trees and chaparral vegetation, descending toward the San Joaquin Valley. To the south, and down more than 5,000 vertical feet, the Middle Fork of the Kaweah River threads its rugged canyon. To the east, snowcapped peaks of the Great Western Divide

and the Kaweah Peaks top out on Mount Kaweah, at 13,802 feet. Just out of sight, beyond the divide, the highest mountain in the contiguous forty-eight states, Mount Whitney, reaches 14,494 feet.

Because park roads top out at 7,800 feet of elevation, most people who visit the parks do not experience the alpine country. Above 9,000 feet the harsh climate cannot support tall trees or dense forests. Above about 11,000 feet, *no* trees grow. Here are mostly boulders, rocks, and gravel punctuated with small alpine lakes, meadows, and low-growing shrubs.

The forests, peaks, valleys, lakes, and streams of Sequoia and Kings Canyon national parks provide a sanctuary for such wildlife as black bear, mule deer, and mountain lions and cougar. Marmots and pikas inhabit the mountains. Coyotes, gray fox, bobcats, raccoons, and ringtails patrol the foothills. Decades of fish plantings introduced non-native brown, brook, golden, and cut-throat trout, but rainbow trout and Little Kern golden trout, native to the Sierra's west-slope streams, are being restored.

Muir called the Sierra Nevadas a "gentle wilderness," which it is indeed. Though the mountains can be harsh on the ill-prepared, they offer superb weather for the backpacker, camper, and day hiker. Precipitation comes mostly in the wintertime, and the temperature extremes are generally mild compared with those of many other mountainous habitats. Mineral King Valley, which was added to Sequoia in 1978, provides hiking access to meadows, alpine lakes, and Sierra peaks. Visitors can explore the Giant Forest by taking advantage of over 40 miles of foot trails.

SEQUOIA NATIONAL PARK
Established 1890
402,482 acres

KINGS CANYON
NATIONAL PARK
Established 1940
461,901 acres

Sequoia and Kings Canyon
National Parks
Three Rivers, CA 93271
(209) 565-3134

ABOVE: The last light of the day illuminates a green marsh between two of the Kearsarge lakes, below the Kearsarge Pinnacles, Kings Canyon National Park.

RIGHT: Fin Dome is reflected in a small tarn above Sixty Lakes Basin, Kings Canyon National Park.

Shenandoah National Park

Skyline Drive winds through hardwood forests along the Blue Ridge Mountains, providing vistas of the spectacular landscape of Shenandoah National Park. The park lies astride a beautiful section of the Blue Ridge, which forms the eastern rampart of the Appalachian Mountains between Pennsylvania and Georgia. In the valley to the west is the Shenandoah River, from which the park gets its name, and between the North and South forks of the river is Massanutten, a 40-mile-long mountain. To the east is the rolling Piedmont country.

Most of the rocks that form the Blue Ridge are ancient granitic and metamorphosed volcanic formations, some exceeding 1 billion years of age. By comparison, humans have been associated with this land for about 11,000 years. Native Americans used the land for centuries but left little evidence of their presence. European settlement of the Shenandoah Valley began soon after the first expedition crossed the Blue Ridge in

1716. Many of the settlers came "up river," north to south, from Pennsylvania. By 1800, the lowlands had been settled by farmers, while the rugged mountains were relatively untouched. Later, as valley farmland became scarce, settlement spread into the mountains. The mountain farmers cleared land, hunted wildlife, and grazed sheep and cattle. By the twentieth century, these people had developed cultural traits of their own, born from the harshness and isolation of mountain living. However, the forests were shrinking, game animals were disappearing, the thin mountain soil was wearing out, and people were beginning to leave.

In 1926, Congress authorized the establishment of Shenandoah National Park, though the park was not actually established until 1935. The Commonwealth of Virginia purchased nearly 280 square miles of land to be donated

An easy trail leads down from the Skyline Drive to Dark Hollow Falls.

to the federal government. More than half of the population had left the mountain area, and the remaining residents sold their land or were relocated, with government assistance. In dedicating the park in 1936, President Franklin D. Roosevelt initiated a novel experiment in allowing an overused area to return to a natural state. The Civilian Conservation Corps built recreational facilities, and in 1939 Skyline Drive was completed. Croplands and pastures soon became overgrown with shrubs, locusts, and pines; these in turn were replaced by oak, hickory, and other trees that make up a mature deciduous forest. Now, more than 95 percent of the park is covered by forests with about 100 species of trees. The vegetative regeneration has been so complete that in 1976 Congress designated two-fifths of the park as wilderness. Today the park faces many new challenges, as air quality declines,

forest pests invade, and land-use patterns around the area change. The largest remaining open area is Big Meadows, which is kept in its historically open condition. Here, wildflowers, strawberries, and blueberries attract wildlife and humans.

SHENANDOAH NATIONAL PARK
Established 1935
196,466 acres
Route 3, Box 348
Luray, VA 22835
(703) 999-2266 (recording)
or (703) 999-2299

Deer, bear, bobcat, turkey, and animals that were rare or absent have now returned. Deer and smaller animals are often seen. Bear are found mostly in back-country areas but are occasionally spotted elsewhere. About 200 species of birds have been reported. A few, such as ruffed grouse,

barred owl, and woodpeckers, are permanent residents. More are seen during the warmer months. These include flycatchers, thrushes, and 35 species of warblers. The park is home to several species of salamanders, and 2 species of poisonous snake, the timber rattlesnake and the copperhead, are occasionally reported, as are several harmless species.

Spring begins in March, with the blooming of red maple, serviceberry, and hepatica. Chipmunks and groundhogs appear. The weather may change quickly. The green of leafing trees moves up the ridge at the rate of about 100 feet a day and does not reach the peaks until late May. Wildflowers bloom during April and May, and the large-flowered trillium carpets the forest floor. Pink azalea blooms in late May, followed by mountain laurel in June. Migrating birds in breeding plumage are numerous.

Summer brings a mantle of

deep green to the ridges and hollows. Many birds are nesting, and the catbird, indigo bunting, and towhee abound. Fawns are often seen. The variety of wildflowers increases as the summer progresses, and by late summer they cover the roadsides and open areas. Fall is the season of brilliant colors and crisp days. Many people come to the park to see the fall color, which is usually at its best between October 10 and 25. The southward migration of birds is highlighted by large numbers of hawks moving along the ridge. Most facilities close about November 1, but Skyline Drive remains open. Winter, with its many clear days and lack of leaves, offers the best opportunities for distant views. Visitors can also hike along more than 500 miles of trails that wind through the ridges and valleys, hills and hollows, laced with sparkling streams and waterfalls, of Shenandoah National Park.

Theodore Roosevelt National Park

"I would not have been President had it not been for my experience in North Dakota," Theodore Roosevelt once remarked when reflecting on the influences that affected him throughout his life. Here, too, many of Roosevelt's attitudes about nature and conservation were sharpened and refined.

Roosevelt first came to the badlands in September 1883 to hunt buffalo. Before returning home to New York, he became interested in the cattle business and joined two other men as partners in the Maltese Cross Ranch. The next year he returned and established a second open-range ranch, the Elkhorn, as his own operation while continuing as a Maltese Cross partner. The Elkhorn became his principal residence, a place where he could lead the "strenuous life" that he loved. The

Today, this rugged terrain is home to eagles, mule, and deer. Bison and elk have been recently reintroduced in an effort to repopulate the area with animals lost to hunters and disease. (DAVID MUENCH)

prospect of big-game hunting had initially brought Roosevelt to the West. But when he arrived, the last large herds of bison were gone, having been lost to hide hunters and disease. In other years, when he managed to spend some time in North Dakota, he became more and more alarmed the damage that was being done to the land and its wildlife. He witnessed the virtual destruction of some big-game species. Overgrazing destroyed the grasslands and, with them, the habitats for small mammals and songbirds. Conservation increasingly became one of Roosevelt's major concerns. When he became president in 1901, Roosevelt pursued this interest in natural history by establishing the U.S. Forest Service and by signing the 1906 Antiquities Act, under which he proclaimed eighteen national monuments. He also obtained congressional approval for the establishment of five national parks and fifty-one wildlife refuges, and to set aside land as national forests.

As a conservationist, Theodore Roosevelt was a major figure in American history. Here, in the North Dakota badlands, where many of his personal concerns first gave rise to his later environmental efforts, Roosevelt is remembered with a national park that bears his name and honors the memory of this great conservationist.

**THEODORE ROOSEVELT
NATIONAL PARK
Established 1978
70,447 acres
P.O. Box 7
Medora, ND 58645
(701) 623-4466**

The rugged landscape of the North Dakota badlands had a history long before Roosevelt set foot here. About 60 million years ago, streams carried eroded materials eastward from the young Rocky Mountains and deposited them on a vast lowland – today's Great Plains. During the warm, rainy periods that followed, dense vegetation grew, fell into swampy areas, and was later buried by new layers of sediments. Eventually this plant material turned into lignite coal. Some plantlife became petrified; today considerable amounts of petrified wood are exposed in the badlands. Bentonite, the blue-gray layer of clay, may be traced to ash from ancient volcanoes far to the west. But even as sediments were being deposited, streams were starting to cut down through the soft strata and to sculpt the infinite variety of buttes, tablelands, and valleys that make up the badlands we know today.

Though at first glance this landscape appears inhospitable and barren, it is home to a great variety of creatures and plants. Rainfall, scant though it is, nourishes the grasses that cover the land. And when the wildflowers bloom in bright profusion, they add their vibrant colors to the reds, browns, and greens of earth and grass. Wood's rose is one of a great number of wildflowers that delighted Roosevelt. At home here, too, are more than 200 species of birds, many of which are songbirds. The floodplain forest, woody draws, sagebrush flats, and grasslands are habitats that support a variety of birds. Visitors can thrill to their songs today as much as Roosevelt did. "One of our sweetest, loudest songsters," he wrote, "is the meadowlark. The Plains air seems to give it a voice and it will perch on top of a bush or tree and sing for hours in rich, bubbling tones." Golden eagles nest in the badlands, feeding on small mammals such as prairie dogs and rabbits. Bald eagles are seen only rarely. Both mule deer and white-tailed deer inhabit the park. The white-tails prefer the river woodlands, and the mule deer like the more broken country and the uplands. Prairie dogs, historically a staple food source for many predators, live in "towns" in the grasslands. Through careful management, some animals that nearly became extinct are once again living here. Bison and elk, for example, were reintroduced in 1956 and 1985, respectively.

Virgin Islands National Park

Visitors can expect to see lush tropical forests brimming with flowers and wildlife.
(NATIONAL PARK SERVICE)

Rumor has it that pirates buried fortunes throughout the Caribbean. Today's visitors to Virgin Islands National Park find treasures of greater value than gold and silver. Awaiting discovery are a wealth of white, sandy beaches fringed by lush green hills, calm turquoise bays, coral reefs surrounded by tropical fish, and remnants of the island's colonial past in Danish sugar plantations.

Just over half of the small rugged volcanic island of St. John is protected as a natural paradise within Virgin Islands National Park (the park's boundaries encompass three-quarters of the island, but the park owns only a little more than half of the island). St. John boasts tropical forests, brilliantly colored wildflowers, and a surprising variety of wildlife within its small borders – the island is only 9 miles long and 5 miles wide. The island's remarkable variety of more than 800 species of plants includes the teyer palm, which is St. John's only

native palm tree; the bay rum tree, whose aromatic leaves once provided the oil for the world-famous bay rum cologne; and rare, brilliantly colored wild orchids. St. John is a sanctuary for animals as diverse as corals, sea turtles, and reef fish; bats; frogs; gecko, anole, and iguana lizards; and more than twenty species of tropical birds. Forests were cleared over almost all of St. John for sugar plantations, farms, and houses in the 1700s and 1800s. Foreign trees and shrubs, brought in to provide food or medicines, invaded the native forests, and, by the early 1900s, no sizable original stands were left. Animals, too, were introduced by man. Some, such as the weasel-like mongoose, which developed a taste for the eggs of ground-nesting birds and sea turtles, have had devastating effects.

Today, with an ample part of St. John's natural resources managed by the park, the tropical forest and much of the island's native wildlife are protected from the effects of development. The park preserves picture-postcard beaches that fringe Hawksnest Bay, Trunk Bay, Cinnamon Bay, Little Lameshur Bay, and many of St. John's other sheltered coves.

Edging parts of the island, between terrestrial and marine ecosystems, lie the ecologically important mangrove communities. Red mangroves, with their distinctive prop roots, occur in shoreline areas where reefs or bays afford protection from waves. Undersea meadows of seagrass beds also prefer these calmer waters. Mangroves and seagrass beds provide food and shelter to an astonishing variety of organisms. The submerged prop roots of the mangroves are encrusted with a colorful assortment of algae, tunicates, sponges, anemones, hydroids, barnacles, and oysters. Secure from predators, juvenile snappers, grunts, groupers, doctorfish, and sardines find shelter amid the maze of roots. When larger, many of them venture out to spend the rest of their lives on the coral reef.

Turtle grass and manatee grass predominate in the seagrass beds. Their gently undulating blades provide food for sea turtles, fish, and sea urchins. Roaming throughout this area are such unusual animals as sea cucumbers, batfish, spotted eagle rays, gold-spotted eels, and queen conch.

Virgin Islands National Park was founded in 1956 after Rockefeller interests bought and donated land on St. John for a national park. The park's boundaries were enlarged in 1962 to include 5,650 acres of submerged lands. This underwater world attracts snorkelers and divers to the kaleidoscope of changing colors; the variety of unusual shapes; and the diversity of coral, fish, and other marine life. Reefs have been compared to underwater cities. Alleys, streets, and cul-de-sacs twist between high-rise coralline structures where vacant dwellings are virtually nonexistent. Wispy cleaner shrimps dance about to attract their more-than-willing finned hosts. Moray eels, spiny lobsters, deflated porcupinefish, and crimson squirrelfish spend their days holed up in reef crevices. At night, the city is transformed into an eerie netherworld in which octopuses slither about and parrotfish seek protection in their veil-like mucus cocoons. Coral polyps emerge from stony skeletal homes, stretching their tentacles out to feast on plankton.

The nearly five centuries of the Virgin Islands' cultural history is just as colorful as the array of wildlife here. Humans inhabited

VIRGIN ISLANDS NATIONAL PARK
Authorized 1956
14,689 acres
6310 Estate Nazareth
Charlotte Amalie, VI 00802
(809) 776-6450

the area long before Columbus's arrival. Archaeological discoveries show that Indians, migrating northward in canoes from South America, lived on St. John as early as 710 B.C. Like most of its Caribbean neighbors, the island later (c. A.D. 300) supported a small population of Arawak Indians, who chose sheltered bays for villages, made pottery, and practiced agriculture.

No lasting settlements were in place until the 1720s. Attracted by lucrative prospects of cultivating sugar cane, the Danes took formal possession in 1694 and raised Denmark's colors in 1718, thereby establishing the first permanent European settlement on St. John at Estate Carolina in Coral Bay. Rapid expansion followed, and by 1733 virtually all of St. John was taken up by 109 cane and cotton plantations. As the economy grew, so did the demand for slaves. Many who were captured in West Africa were of tribal nobility and former slaveowners themselves. In 1733, they revolted, and an island-wide massacre of families occurred. Six months passed before the rebellion was quelled.

The emancipation of slaves in 1848 was one of several factors that led to the decline of St. John's plantations. By the early twentieth century, cattle and subsistence farming and bay-rum production were the main industries.

The United States purchased the islands in 1917, and by the 1930s the seed of a tourism industry had sprouted. The founding of Virgin Islands National Park in 1956 now protects some of St. John's spectacular natural features from overdevelopment.

Voyageurs National Park

The only way to explore Voyageurs National Park – which encompasses more than thirty lakes dotted with forested islands – is to ply the waters by boat, as was done in the heyday of the fur trade by the French-Canadian canoemen, or "voyageurs," for whom the park is named. Bordering Canada, this Minnesota park protects the eastern timber wolf, bald eagle, and other wildlife inhabiting the forests, bogs, marshes, beaver ponds, and other natural habitats.

As the fur trade of the late eighteenth and early nineteenth centuries expanded westward, it depended heavily upon the voyageurs, who moved beaver and other pelts and trade goods between Montreal and the Canadian Northwest. The route of these adventuresome men, who paddled up to sixteen hours per day, became so established that the 1783 treaty ending the American

Voyageurs' forests are natural habitats for many animals. (DAVID MUENCH)

Revolution specified that the international boundary should follow their "customary waterway" between Lake Superior and Lake of the Woods. Today, Voyageurs National Park, established in 1975, adjoins a 56-mile stretch of that voyageurs' highway.

Voyageurs risked their lives to advance the fur trade. The enemy took the form of rival fur company representatives, unfriendly Indians, or Nature's forces. They came to know the country well, and they, along with the Indians and lumberjacks, gave this region the bulk of its place-names, such as Grassy Portage, Kabetogama Lake, and Cutover Island.

The landscape of Voyageurs National Park still bears the elements of the fur trade. The waters provided the "highway"; fur-bearing animals provided the goods; and the boundless forests provided the materials for the birch-bark canoe. The canoes were constructed of birch bark, cedar boughs, and cedar or spruce root bindings sealed with pitch. This skill at canoe-making, developed by the Native Americans, was readily exploited by early European explor-

ers. The canoes were light, easily navigable, and quickly repaired with native materials. For several generations the fur trade was the continent's biggest industry, returning investments up to twentyfold.

The park, which lies in the southern portion of the Canadian Shield, has a long geologic history.

VOYAGEURS NATIONAL PARK
Established 1975
218,035 acres
3131 Highway 53
International Falls, MN 56649
(218) 283-9821

The ancient sediments that compose the shield represent some of the oldest rock formations exposed anywhere in the world. Younger rock formations do not appear here. Perhaps they never existed, but more likely glaciation simply removed them. In the past 1 million years, continental glaciers – ice sheets 2 miles thick – bulldozed their way through the area. They removed previous features, leaving mostly level, pock-marked rock up to 2.7 billion years old. Hundreds

of ponds, lakes, and streams now nestle in the depressions, and some rock surfaces in the park still bear the scrape marks. The glaciers gouged out the lake- and riverbeds and set the stage for vast forests.

This watery landscape provides habitats rich with wildlife. Osprey, eagle, and great blue heron nests exist throughout the park. Observant visitors likely will see kingfishers, mergansers, loons, and cormorants. Since water covers one-third of the surface of the park, aquatic animals are common. Creating ponds, the beaver provides not only its own habitat but also the environment needed by aquatic plants. These plants provide food for aquatic insects and some fish. The fish, in turn, support the wide variety of fish-eating birds. And beaver are fare for coyotes and timber wolves.

Perhaps nothing so symbolizes Voyageurs National Park's enduring primitive character as the presence of its wolves. The park is in the heart of the only region in the continental United States where the eastern timber wolf survives. Wolves are shy and secretive, and contrary to folklore they pose vir-

tually no threat to humans. Their wariness and small numbers make it unlikely that visitors will see them, although their tracks in winter may be traced. Wolves usually live in packs of two to twelve. The timber wolf may cover as many as 40 miles in a single night and can run for several miles at speeds of 30 to 35 miles per hour.

Winter in Voyageurs National Park is a force to be reckoned with. From spring thaw until freeze-up, the voyageurs had six months at most to complete their travel. Their round-trip between depots at Grand Portage or Fort William on Lake Superior and the subarctic interior of northwest Canada consumed four or five months.

Summer is relatively short here, but winter need not be a time of inactivity. Ski travel is often possible as snow blankets both land and lake. And warming temperatures and crusted snow in late winter definitely invite snowshoers.

When the waterways begin to open in spring, animals stir from a season's rest. It's one of the best times to observe Nature here. For many, the display of fall colors in the park is the highlight of the year.

Wind Cave National Park

Herds of bison thrive in the lands around the Wind Cave. (NATIONAL PARK SERVICE)

When the first settlers in the area, Jesse and Tom Bingham, discovered the Wind Cave in 1881, drawn to a small hole in the ground by a loud whistling noise, the wind was said to be blowing with such force out of the cave's opening that it knocked Jesse's hat off. That wind, which gave the cave its name, is created by differences between atmospheric pressures in and outside the cave.

It was left to later adventurers like Alvin McDonald to follow that wind and discover the cave's extensive network of passageways containing "boxwork," "popcorn," and "frostwork" formations, and other delicate irreplaceable features. Young Alvin, and others who explored the cave before the turn of the century, were fascinated by what they found – chocolate-colored crystals, formations resembling faces or animals, and chambers that inspired names such as the "Garden of Eden" and the "Dungeon."

Reports of these discoveries drew a stream of curious tourists to the cave. Local entrepreneurs, including the McDonald family, blasted open passages and guided tourists through for a fee. Cave specimens were removed and sold. The cave's more than 70 miles of passageways have been protected since 1903, when the Wind Cave became America's seventh national park.

Don't be fooled by the park's name. There is much more to Wind Cave National Park than its underground geological formations. A diverse mix of wildlife, including bison, pronghorn, and prairie dogs, swell in the 28,292 acres of rolling grasslands, pine forests, hills, and ravines that cover its sunlit upper layer. Here you can see a small remnant of the prairie and begin to imagine the scene that greeted westward-bound nineteenth-century pioneers – not farms and cities, as today, but open plains stretching across the middle of the continent. A piece of that prairie is preserved here in an almost natural state.

Vast open prairies can look deceptively empty. But take a closer look. A small dark shape on the horizon may actually be a bison grazing knee-deep in bluestem and other grasses. You may glimpse a well-camouflaged coyote hunting among the prairie-dog towns. Slowly comes the realization that the nutrient-rich plants of the plains support an abundance of wildlife. When Wind Cave National Park was first established, its main purpose was to protect the cave. But, by 1912, the protection and re-establishment of native wildlife within the park's boundaries were recognized as an equally important goal.

Among the park's foremost missions as a wildlife sanctuary was the restoration of populations of bison, elk, and pronghorn to the Black Hills of South Dakota. By the late 1880s, these animals had been eliminated from this part of their range, largely as a result of uncontrolled hunting. The story of the bison's return reflects the success of the park's management programs. Starting with 14 bison donated by the Bronx Zoo in 1913, the herd numbers about 350 today.

Other wildlife, including mule deer, cottontail rabbits, and many kinds of birds, lives in the prairies, forests, and hills of Wind Cave. Located near the middle of the country, the park embraces animal and plant species common to both the East and West. Don't be sur-prised to see ponderosa pines and pinyon jays – both western natives – alongside American elms and eastern bluebirds.

WIND CAVE NATIONAL PARK
Established 1903
28,292 acres
R.R. 1, Box 190
Hot Springs, SD 57747
(605) 745-4600

The Wind Cave has a long geological history predating its discovery by the Binghams. One of the world's oldest caves, the formation began some 320 million years ago. At that time parts of the limestone that constitute the upper levels of Wind Cave were being dissolved into cave passageways. As ancient ocean levels fluctuated, these passages were filled with sediments. Beneath the ocean, a thick layer of sediments continued to be deposited above that limestone.

About 60 million years ago, the forces that uplifted the Rocky Mountains also uplifted the modern Black Hills, producing large fractures and cracks in the overlying limestone. Over millions of years, water moving slowly through those cracks dissolved the limestone to produce the complex maze of the cave's passages.

Later erosion changed surface drainage patterns, which caused subsurface water levels to drop, draining the cave passages. As the modern Wind Cave formed, many of these newer passages intersected the original cave, revealing the red clay and sandstone sediments from 320 million years ago.

It was after the cave formed that most of the colorful cave formations began to decorate its walls. One of the most prominent features in Wind Cave is boxwork – thin, honeycomb-shaped structures of calcite that protrude from the walls and ceilings. Some of the better-known cave formations, such as stalactites and stalagmites, are uncommon here.

Despite 100 years of exploration, only an estimated 5 percent of the cave has been discovered. In 1891, Alvin McDonald wrote in a diary of his cave trips: "Have given up the idea of finding the end of Wind Cave." The better-equipped cavers of today have not given up. They are continuing to push farther and farther into the cave's cool, black recesses.

Wrangell–St. Elias National Park and Preserve

Autumn colors brighten the slopes above the Chitina Valley.

the sixteen highest American peaks, including Mount St. Elias, the second-highest peak, at 18,008 feet.

But Wrangell–St. Elias, which lies a day's drive from Anchorage in south-central Alaska, is more than peaks, glaciers, and rivers. It provides a protected habitat for diverse Alaskan wildlife and preserves old mining sites left behind as reminders of man's early explorations here.

Adventuresome visitors come to Wrangell–St. Elias to hike the mountains, ski across the glaciers, or paddle the rivers. The scarcity of roads means that many travelers will not enter the park itself, but even then some of its major peaks, including Blackburn, Sanford, Drum, and Wrangell, can be seen from nearby highways.

Four major mountain ranges meet here: the Wrangells huddle in the northern interior; the Chugach guard the southern coast; the St. Elias Mountains rise abruptly from the Gulf of Alaska,

The astounding size of Wrangell–St. Elias National Park and Preserve stands unrivaled. Six times the size of Yellowstone National Park, it is the largest national park in the United States.

Often referred to as the "mountain kingdom of North America," the park and preserve boast nine of thrusting northward past the Chugach and on toward the Wrangells; and the eastern end of the Alaskan Range, mapped as the Nutzotin and Mentasta mountains, forms part of the preserve's northern boundary. The Wrangells are volcanic in origin, but only Mount Wrangell remains active, with vents of steam near its summit. The last reported eruption was in 1900. With adjoining Kluane National Park in Canada, all these ranges form the premier mountain wilderness in North America. The high country is covered with snow year-round, resulting in extensive icefields and glaciers. The Bagley Icefield near the coast is the largest subpolar icefield in North America and spawns such giant glaciers as the Tana, Miles, Hubbard, and Guyot. The Malaspina Glacier flows out of the St. Elias Range between Icy Bay and Yakutat Bay in a mass larger than the state of Rhode

Island. It carries so much glacial silt that plants and trees take hold on its extremities, grow to maturity, and topple over the edge as the glacier melts.

WRANGELL–ST. ELIAS NATIONAL PARK AND PRESERVE
Established 1980
National park:
8,331,604 acres
National preserve:
4,856,721 acres
P.O. Box 29
Glennallen, AK 99588
(907) 822-5234

Flowing from the glaciers are a multitude of meandering rivers and braided streams. The Copper River, the largest, forms the western boundary of the park, starting in the Wrangells and emptying into the Gulf of Alaska in

Chugach National Forest. In the early 1900s the Kennicott Mining Co. transported copper from its mines near McCarthy by railroad, along the Chitina and Copper rivers, to ships at Cordova. Ore was extracted from these highly productive mines between 1911 and 1938 and lured many people to the area. During that period, gold was extracted from the Nabesna area as well. Today mining still occurs on private lands within the park, and you can see evidence of earlier mining, including the ruins of the Kennicott mines, which have been placed on the National Register of Historic Places. Indian villages expanded and a number of new towns sprang up in mining's heyday. Copper Center, Chitina, Gulkana, and Chistochina are among the old Athapascan settlements. Yakutat, on the coast, is a traditional Tlingit fishing village.

Though the vegetation may seem sparse, especially in the interior, the park contains a variety of wildlife. Dall's sheep and mountain goats patrol the craggy peaks. Herds of caribou feed on the lichen and low woody plants around the Wrangells. Moose browse in sloughs and bogs in the coastal lowlands and in brushy areas, which also attract brown and grizzly bears. Black bears roam throughout the park. Bison were released in the Copper and Chitina river valleys in 1950 and 1962, respectively, and remain as separate herds today. Many rivers, streams, and lakes provide spawning grounds for salmon and other fish. The Copper River drainage and the Malaspina forelands are major flyways for migratory birds and include prime nesting sites for trumpeter swans. Sea lions, harbor seals, and other marine mammals can be spotted along the coastal areas of the park.

Yellowstone National Park

The eruptions of Old Faithful and some 10,000 other geysers and hot springs are but some of the impressive natural forces that draw visitors from around the world to Yellowstone National Park. At the heart of Yellowstone's past, present, and future lies volcanism. About 2 million years ago, then 1.2 million years ago, and then again 600,000 years ago, catastrophic volcanic eruptions occurred here. The latest eruption spewed out nearly 240 cubic miles of debris. What is now the park's central portion then collapsed, forming a 28-by-47-mile caldera, or basin. The magmatic heat powering those eruptions still powers the park's famous geysers, hot springs, fumaroles, and mud pots.

Bigger than the states of Delaware and Rhode Island combined, Yellowstone is the largest national park in the lower forty-eight states, encompassing more than 2,200,000 acres and spanning parts of Wyoming, Idaho, and Montana. Established in 1872, it is also the world's first national park.

Yellowstone preserves an unparalleled array of geothermal phenomena. Geysers are created as surface water seeps down into porous rock layers to be heated under pressure and then rises back up as geysers or hot springs. As superheated water nears the surface, pressure drops and it flashes into the steam of a geyser. Hot springs occur when water emerges that is not superheated or under pressure. Fumaroles, lacking enough moisture to flow, vent steam. Mud pots form over fumaroles, whose acid gases decompose rocks into mud and clay.

The park's major scenic attractions are located along the Grand Loop Road, the roughly figure-eight–shaped, 142-mile road in the center of the park. Other sites can be explored along the park's 1,000 miles of trails. Many of the most famous geysers and hot springs are located on the west side of the park, along the 50-mile stretch of road between Mammoth Hot

Twice as high as Niagara, the Lower Falls in the Grand Canyon of the Yellowstone River is one of the most spectacularly situated waterfalls in North America.

Springs and Old Faithful. Attractions include the Mammoth Hot Springs Terraces, Norris Geyser Basin, Fountain Paint Pot, Firehole Lake Drive, Midway Geyser Basin, Biscuit Basin, Black Sand Basin – and Old Faithful, the world's best-known geyser.

In Black Sand Basin, the bright colors of Sunset Lake and Emerald Pool attract photographers. At Biscuit Basin, mineral deposits took on biscuit shapes before a 1959 earthquake triggered changes, destroying the formations. Norris Geyser Basin's array of thermal features is unparalleled. Steamboat Geyser, the world's largest, erupts at irregular intervals of days to years. Echinus Geyser is more predictable – it erupts about once per hour. Porcelain Basin is Yellowstone's hottest exposed area. At Mammoth Hot Springs, the terraces are spectacular travertine (calcium carbonate) formations deposited daily. Most new rock from Yellowstone's geysers is called "geyserite," a non-crystalline mineral chemically similar to glass.

The spectacular Grand Canyon of the Yellowstone River, which extends from the Canyon Village area to Tower Junction and plunges 1,000 feet below, provides a glimpse of Earth's interior: its waterfalls highlight the boundaries of lava flows and thermal areas. The spectacular 308-foot Lower Falls, almost twice the height of Niagara Falls, can be admired from such viewpoints as Grandview Point, Lookout Point, and Artist Point. A trail leads to Upper Falls View, where one can see the shorter but no less stunning 109-foot Upper Falls. Tower Falls, tumbling 132 feet, was named for the adjacent volcanic pinnacles.

The canyon's hues of yellow and orange were created by hot water acting on volcanic rock. It was not these colors but the river's yellow banks at its distant confluence with the Missouri River that occasioned the Minnetaree Indian name that French trappers translated as *roche jaune*, "yellow stone." The canyon has been rapidly downcut more than once, perhaps by great glacier outburst floods. Little deepening takes place today.

Rugged mountains flank the park's volcanic plateau, rewarding both eye and spirit. South from Tower Falls, as you drive up Mount Washburn, you can look east, downslope, into prime grizzly bear country on Antelope Creek. This area is closed to visitors to offer the bears refuge. Apart from grizzly and black bears, bison, moose, and elk roam Yellowstone's vast terrain. The best times to see wild animals in summer are early morning and late evening. The Lewis River environs near the South Entrance are good elk and moose habitat. Elk, bison, pronghorn, and coyotes may be spotted in Lamar Valley, and pronghorn can be found in sagebrush flats near the North Entrance. Bighorn sheep frequent Mount Washburn in summer. Watch for mule deer near Old Faithful, Yellowstone Lake, the Grand Canyon of Yellowstone, and the areas between the North Entrance and Tower.

Yellowstone Lake – measuring 20 miles long, 14 miles wide, and up to 320 feet deep – is North America's largest mountain lake above 7,000 feet. Rich shrubland around the lake provides food for a variety of wild birds and animals. Waterfowl, including white pelicans and trumpeter swans, abound along Yellowstone River, which flows out of Yellowstone Lake and meanders through the Hayden Valley. Fishing Bridge, which was closed to fishing in 1973, spans the Yellowstone River and now offers one of the best wild trout-spawning shows anywhere for most of the summer. The Hayden Valley, between Fishing Bridge and Canyon, and Pelican Creek, east of Fishing Bridge, is moose and bison territory.

Yellowstone's history resonates with colorful tales of fur trappers, explorers and surveyors, with their photographers and artists. William Henry Jackson's photographs and Thomas Moran's sketches influenced Congress to establish Yellowstone in 1872. The park has since been recognized as an International Biosphere Reserve and World Heritage Site as well.

YELLOWSTONE NATIONAL PARK
Established 1872
2,219,791 acres
P.O. Box 168
Yellowstone National Park, WY 82190
(Also in Montana and Idaho)
(307) 344-7381

The frosty appearance of deposits at Mammoth Hot Springs belies their steaming hot origin.

Brightly colored algae thrive in the scalding run off from the hot springs in the Norris Geyser Basin.

Yosemite National Park

Clouds Rest and Half Dome at sunset from the glaciated, granite slopes above Olmsted Point.

Yosemite National Park embraces granite peaks and domes that rise high above broad meadows in the heart of the Sierra Nevadas, which stretch along California's eastern flank. Thousands of visitors flock to Yosemite each day to explore its alpine wilderness, the groves of giant sequoias, and Yosemite Valley. The 196 miles of roads give access to these areas by car, but to get to know the real Yosemite, you must leave your car and stroll along some of the park's 800 miles of trails.

Tuolumne Meadows, at 8,600 feet, is the largest subalpine meadow in the Sierras, featuring some of the most rugged, sublime scenery. In summer the meadows, lakes, and exposed granite slopes teem with life. Because of the short growing season, the plants and animals take maximum advantage of the warm days to grow, reproduce, and store food for the winter ahead.

Tuolumne Meadows is 55 miles from Yosemite Valley via the Tioga Road, which passes through this terrain of sparkling lakes, fragile meadows, domes, and lofty peaks that only 10,000 years ago lay under glacial ice. Overlooks along the road afford superb views. At

YOSEMITE NATIONAL PARK
Established 1890
761,236 acres
P.O. Box 577
Yosemite National Park, CA
95389
(209) 372-0200

Tioga Pass the road crosses the Sierras' crest, at 9,945 feet, the highest automobile pass in California.

Long a focal point of summer activity, Tuolumne Meadows is growing in popularity as a winter mountaineering area. In the summer it is a favorite starting point for backpacking trips and day hikes. The meadows are spectacular in early summer, abounding in wildflowers and wildlife.

Glacier Point is one of those rare places where the scenery is so vast that it overwhelms the viewer. Below, a sheer rock cliff about 3,200 feet straight down affords you a bird's-eye view of the entire Yosemite Valley. Across the valley you can see the 2,425-foot drop of Yosemite Falls. Beyond, the panoramic expanse of the High Sierras stands out in awe-inspiring

clarity. In summer you can drive to Glacier Point, 32 miles from Yosemite Valley. In winter, when the road is closed at Badger Pass Ski Area, Glacier Point is a favorite destination for cross-country skiers.

Yosemite Valley is probably the best-known example of a glacier-carved canyon. Its leaping waterfalls, towering cliffs, rounded domes, and massive monoliths make it a pre-eminent natural marvel that has inspired poets, painters, photographers, and such conservationists as John Muir.

Yosemite Valley is characterized by sheer walls and a flat floor. Its evolution began when alpine glaciers lumbered through the canyon of the Merced River. The ice carved through weaker sections of granite, scouring rock but leaving intact harder portions, such as El Capitan and Cathedral rocks. The glacier greatly enlarged the canyon that the Merced River had carved through successive uplifts of the Sierras. Finally the glacier began to melt, and the terminal moraine left by the last glacial advance into the valley dammed the melting water to form ancient Lake Yosemite, which sat in the newly carved U-

shaped valley. Sediment eventually filled in the lake, forming the flat floor seen today. This process is now filling Mirror Lake at the base of Half Dome.

The valley is a mosaic of open meadows sprinkled with wildflowers and flowering shrubs, oak woodlands, and mixed-conifer forests of ponderosa pine, incense-cedar, and Douglas fir. Wildlife, from monarch butterflies to mule deer and black bears, flourishes in these communities. Waterfalls around the valley's perimeter reach their maximum flow in May and June, and crash to the floor. Yosemite, Bridalveil, Vernal, Nevada, and Illilouette are the most prominent falls, some of which have little or no water from mid-August through early fall.

The Mariposa Grove, 35 miles south of Yosemite Valley, is the largest of three sequoia groves in Yosemite. The Tuolumne and Merced groves are near Crane Flat. Despite human pressures, these towering trees, largest of all living things, have endured for thousands of years. The Mariposa Grove's Grizzly Giant, 2,700 years old, is thought to be the oldest living sequoia. Only in recent years have we begun to understand the giant-sequoia environment. During the last 100 years, protection has sometimes been inadequate and sometimes excessive. For example, in the late 1800s, tunnels were cut through two trees in the Mariposa Grove. Conversely, good intentions created another problem: protection from fire has resulted in adverse effects.

Sequoias are wonderfully adapted to fire. The wood and bark are fire-resistant. Black scars on a number of large trees still prospering indicate they have survived many scorching fires. Sequoia reproduction also depends on fire – seeds require mineral soil for germination, and seedlings need sunlight. Historically, frequent natural fires opened the forest, thinned out competing plant species, and left rich mineral soil behind. But years of fire suppression have resulted in debris, such as fallen branches, accumulating, stifling reproduction, and allowing shade-tolerant trees to encroach. Prescribed fires, intended to simulate natural fires and improve the health of the forest, are now set by the National

Park Service.

For a taste of Yosemite's pioneer past, visit the Pioneer Yosemite History Center, a collection of relocated historic buildings and horse-drawn coaches. Wawona, where the center is located, was once an Indian encampment and, later, the site of a wayside hotel built in 1857 by Galen Clark. Known as "Clark's Station," it served as a stop for visitors in transit between Yosemite Valley and Mariposa. In 1864, when Yosemite Valley and the Mariposa Grove were set aside for protection (Yosemite National Park was later established in 1890), Clark became the first guardian of the area. In 1875, the year the original Wawona road opened, the Washburn brothers purchased the area and built the Wawona Hotel that is still in operation today. Exhibits at the Valley Visitor Center highlight the valley's natural and human history. Nearby, the Indian Cultural Museum displays the cultural history of the native Miwok and Paiute people from 1850 to the present, and the Museum Gallery features artwork of past and current Yosemite artists.

ABOVE: Cathedral Rocks in the late afternoon, viewed from a meadow in Yosemite Valley

LEFT: The Merced River thunders over the 594-foot-high Nevada Falls during the spring run off.

Zion National Park

The White Cliffs tower above the striated sandstone near the eastern boundary of the park.

"There is an eloquence to their forms which stirs the imagination with a singular power and kindles in the mind…. Nothing can exceed the wondrous beauty of Zion," wrote geologist Clarence E. Dutton in 1880 of this sculptured landscape. When Dutton wrote this description, southern Utah was a wild, rugged country of little-known canyons and plateaus. Slowly, scientific reports, magazine articles, and photographs spread the word that deep within this remote territory lay the scenic phenomenon of Zion.

Protected within Zion National Park are massive multicolored vertical cliffs, deep canyons, waterfalls, hoodoos – weird, iron-capped rocks resembling enormous mushrooms – and Kolob Arch – perhaps the world's largest arch, spanning 310 feet. This landscape so impressed nineteenth-century Mormon settlers that they named it "Zion," "the heavenly city of God."

Today's explorers can drive

through the park's spectacular cliff-and-canyon landscape. Sheer, vividly colored cliffs tower above Zion Canyon Scenic Drive, which follows the floor of Zion Canyon. This narrow, deep canyon, with 2,000- to 3,000-foot high walls, is the centerpiece of the park. Along the bottom of the canyon flows the Virgin River, with the looks of a creek and the muscle of the Colorado. This small river almost singlehandedly carved the profound rock gorge of Zion Canyon. It began its downcutting more than 13 million years ago and continues its work today. You may witness the river's power during a flash flood, when it turns muddy and violent, whisking away cottonwoods and boulders as if they were twigs and pebbles.

On most days, though, the Virgin winds through the canyon peacefully. Fremont cottonwoods, willows, and velvet ashes along its banks provide shady spots for a picnic or a short walk. Mule deer and many birds, too, seek refuge from the extreme midday heat of summer beneath this canopy. Other wildlife, including ringtail cats, bobcats, foxes, rock squirrels,

and cottontails, rest under rocky ledges. The best times to see animals along the road are early morning, evening, and at night, when they are most active. These are also ideal times to see the conspicuous white trumpet-shaped flowers of the sacred datura. This common roadside plant is also called "moonlily" because its blossoms open in the cooler hours of evening and wilt with the rising heat of the day.

The Zion–Mt. Carmel Highway, completed in 1930, was considered an "almost impossible project," an engineering marvel of its time. Built across rough up-and-down terrain, it connects lower Zion Canyon with the high plateaus to the east. Two narrow tunnels, including one 1,936 yards long, were drilled and blasted through the cliffs to finish the construction job. As you travel from one side of the long tunnel to the other, the landscape changes dramatically. On one side lies Zion Canyon, with its massive cliff walls. The colossal size of the canyon is matched by one of the most striking attractions along this road – the Great Arch of Zion, a

"blind" arch carved high in a vertical cliff wall. On the other side of the tunnel is slickrock country. Here rocks colored white and in pastels of orange and red have been eroded into hundreds of fantastic shapes, etched through time with odd patterns of cracks and grooves. The mountain of sandstone known as Checkerboard Mesa stands as the most prominent example of this naturally sculptured rock art.

Two roads lead into the northwestern corner of the park, where streams have carved spectacular canyons at the edge of the Kolob Terrace. The Kolob Canyons Road penetrates 5 miles into the redrock, perpendicular-walled Finger Canyons, ending at a high viewpoint. The Kolob Terrace Road overlooks the white and salmon-colored cliffs of the Left and Right forks of North Creek. Both routes

ZION NATIONAL PARK
Established 1919
146,598 acres
Springdale, UT 84767
(801) 772-3256

climb into forests of pinyon pine and juniper; ponderosa pine, fir, and quaking aspen are found at Lava Point. In summer there is often a feel of mountain coolness to the air of the Kolob's high-country plateaus. And, in the early spring, the Kolob is buried under a thick snowpack. The sparkling white of the snow heightens the colors of this vivid landscape.

The names of the trails in Zion – Emerald Pools, Hidden Canyon, the Narrows, Canyon Overlook – hint at some of what you can find beyond the road. There are surprises too – a desert swamp, a petrified forest, springs and waterfalls, and the always unpredictable appearance of wildlife. The park is a sanctuary for roadrunners and golden eagles, mule deer and mountain lions, cactus and cottonwood. You may surprise lizards or Gambel's quail on a hike along a wooded wash on the desert's edge. Or hear echoes of the clear gushing song of the canyon wren in a pygmy forest of pinyon pine and juniper. Watch for tracks; they may be the closest you get to rarely seen species like the mountain lion or the nocturnal ringtailed cat.

ABOVE: Cliffs of Navajo sandstone glow in the light before dawn.

LEFT: Orderville Canyon is one of several very deep, sheer-walled "slot" canyons in the park.

Index